YOUR BEST LIFE LATER

FINDING GOD'S WILL
IN FOOTBALL, IN CRISIS, AND IN LIFE

To: Linda ♥

♂ Bailey B. Heard

Andrew B. Heard

Faith over fear

Thank You!

xulon PRESS

www.baileyheard.com
www.andrewbheard.com
www.ellieproject.com

YOUR BEST LIFE LATER

ALSO BY ANDREW B. HEARD

A Gray Faith
The Ellie Project

This book is dedicated to my family.
Without your love and support, this story would not be possible.

A special thanks to Amy Allen for First Edition editing.

A special thanks to Julie Kragen for Second Edition editing.

Table of Contents

§

CHAPTER ONE

Early Evidence

§

"So Samuel took the horn of oil and anointed him in the presence of his brothers, and from that day on the Spirit of the Lord came upon David in power."
-1 Samuel 16:13

It is to be noted while none of us know God completely, He most certainly knows all of us. The pursuit to know God is somewhat hastened as we mature in years, but it is in essence no different than the pursuit we experience as a child. We all chase God, but it is more apparent to certain individuals. A day does not pass I do not want to be loved. A day does not pass I do not want something to admire. It is true a day does not pass in which a person does not desire to be taken care of because in some form or fashion, we are all without. I have never found my neediness in food, yet that does not mean I am not in need of food. Many people are very much in need of food and yet where I am cognizant of my lacking is in love. I thirst for it as a man walking a vast desert and yet I know where the spring lies. For the source of my pursuit in love is the same as the source of the need for provision. I search as a fool for something that is right in front of me. I am reminded of the many times in which I searched for my own sunglasses as they sat atop my very head. We have all looked for the glasses that were on our own heads and during the search, a feeling of great frustration can overwhelm a person to the point of trembling exertion. It is a foolish delight that overwhelms the person who looks with great frustration for the very thing that has been with them for their entire search. Delight comes with discovery, but a fog comes with the frustration of forgetfulness. I am reminded to remember the place on which sits the very thing of which we are all in search.

* * *

My bedroom was on the second floor of my parents' garden home. Our home was a rather large house, especially for the small town in which we lived, but my parents picked it because it did not look as large as it actually was from the street. That is how my parents are, crafty and humble for their position. This is not to say pride has never crept into their lives, as it does us all, but rather that for the great achievements that have taken place in their lives, they have handled their decision-making with tact and grace. Reflecting on our situation, I notice a conscious decision on the part of my parents to present themselves in a humble manner.

I believe this wisdom is from God and I have taken it upon myself to imitate their very wise nature. I am afraid I do not live up to this very lofty task well, but for now it is sufficient to rely on the fact God moves in our character with time and He will move in mine as He sees fit. My bedroom changed many times while I lived in my parents' house, but while I was young, it was in the far southeast corner. My bed was situated under the windows that faced our backyard. Our backyard was full of mystery, because in it sat two rather peculiar oak trees that formed one very large oak tree. These trees are very old, probably over one hundred years, and create quite an impressive feeling.

At age 5, the feeling of impressiveness was more a feeling of terror late at night as the wind whipped through those old oak trees. It was in the night, which was sometimes filled with terror, my encounters with God took place. Our exchange was not audible, for that was never the way in which we talked. It was much more intimate. Words can only carry a person so far. I waited and the euphoric feeling started to take place. It seemed to well up from deep within me and move from the depths of my soul into the forefront of my mind, and there in my mind it settled.

Curled up in a ball on this particular night, the message came to me. As I waited in silence, my mind was swept into a whirlwind of travel and adventure. Pictures of far-off lands came into my head. The only far-off exotic land I had reference to pull up at such a young age was Africa. Africa was all of a sudden at the forefront of my mind, but gone were the feelings of adventure.

Instead, feelings of disconnection with my family and sacrifice were so prevalent on my heart I thought it would burst. Later in my life, I would come to realize God was calling me to surrender to the ministry, however at the age of 5, I did not know or understand the details of His message. The deeper meaning, however, was clear: He wanted me to go and I wanted to stay.

I argued with Him mightily, asking, *Father, why would You ask me to go so far away? Are there no other people to do these things? Is it not enough I love You? You must not really want me to leave my family, because You know I love You and I could be of such great help here. I could be great for You, Father, only let me be great here! I would be willing to be great for You! So what is it You really want me to do?*

A feeling of ease quieted my soul as I finally proposed the right question and stopped demanding a certain answer. I waited for the response with careful patience, because this discourse was not something uncommon to me at this age. The answer I received, however, was too scary for me to accept.

No, it cannot be, I protested. *You cannot ask me to do such a thing. I will not leave my family to spread Your Word. It is too much for me to bear!*

With the word *too*, I burst into tears as only one who knows the receiver of the tears so well. They expressed my emotion and my need for sympathy in ways I did not have the power to muster otherwise. I was crushed with grief and fear. I was not yet old enough to know resentment, but it was starting to give birth in the depths of my heart. Was this love? Surely, it was not. I was young, but I did not think this could possibly be love. To be so close with someone, to spend so much time together, and then to have Him ask me to do something that was so much against my will. Surely this request placed upon my heart was not what was desired.

If a person is not acquainted with my God, then he or she may not understand the form through which my answers always came. It is the most cherished form of communication and I wish it was common to only me, but I am afraid I cannot claim it as mine alone. It is shared by many, but those people who experience it find it is as if it were only He and they who ever spoke in such a way. One's soul and His are somehow intertwined and through this connection, He is able to bring the pictures and emotions of the message He communicates. It is not like human communication where there may be a misunderstanding because of the words people used and the perceived emotions at the time.

Some people have said there have been misunderstandings of His messages in the past, but I think it is more accurate to say the message was received without error and then disobeyed. Disobedience must be the answer, for when He speaks He uses one's own words and one's own emotions. Words are not even necessary except in the processing, for the message comes, so many times, in vision.

But, back to our argument. My pleas for reconsideration regarding sending me so far away continued after some sobbing, *Father, I love You, but I love my family so very much. Please do not force me to leave them. Do not let them be taken from me.*

At that time, I knew no stronger love on earth than the love that my family had given me the first five years of my life, and I was so afraid to lose it. A young child depends on family so much and when one's family was as good and kind as mine had been, the attachment to them is even greater. I was torn between His love and their love. My argument with God would continue on in different forms until well into my teenage years, when the truth of serving Him, as opposed to serving the ideals my peer group and society preached, would become undeniable.

$$\star \star \star$$

As a child, God's love had come on me like a flood, and I had no time to think on it except to be swept away by it. I do not remember a time in which I did not feel His heart upon my heart. I know this is not true for everyone and I do not know why it was true for me, but my heart cannot deny it. The time in which one begins to remember the happenings of life is hard to pinpoint, to say the least, but my earliest memories contain Him in the midst of them. He was not there outlined in great detail as adults outline other people, but He was there as the heat of a fireplace is there in a cozy television room on a cold night. I felt Him in my bones, and the impression of Him is stamped on my memory in ways which I am not eloquent enough to articulate.

The feeling etched in my memory so well was formally solidified during my fifth year of life as well. The process of that solidification came about in this manner:

It was early Sunday morning as my family and I pulled into the jailhouse parking lot. The jail parking lot was where we always parked, as it was right across the street from our church. We pulled into a parking space slanted for easy parking, and as I got out of the car, the feeling of His presence began to become apparent to me. This did not alarm me, for his presence was common and a child does not fear what is common and good. As I walked, He began to talk and a sensation of delight took hold of my heart.

Andrew, you know who I am, He said. *Now it is time others know you know Me as well.*

I did not tell my mother of the conversation as we walked into the church. I do not know why I did not inform her, other than the fact it did not seem necessary. I walked into my church's sanctuary with one motive in mind. My church was a Baptist church and there was a customary invitation at the end of every service. This was an opportunity to receive Jesus Christ as one's Savior and Lord. I knew this invitation period was a given, and so I intended to make my relationship with God known during this time.

The service proceeded as usual, and much to my now-older mind's perplexity, I was not in the least nervous. My proclamation in front of hundreds of people seemed a perfectly natural thing to do. As the service neared the end, the invitation was extended and, much to the astonishment of my mother, I got up and walked down the aisle. As I approached the preacher, I addressed him in a simple fashion. "I would like to receive Jesus Christ into my heart," I said.

I knew Him already and I was completely aware of His Lordship due to our previous conversations and the actions of my parents. I was raised in Bible School from the time I was old enough to slap on pajamas and boots. Pajamas and boots were, of course, my normal fashion to preschool Bible School. I suppose I was a trendsetter from the start. In pajamas and boots, I learned all the stories of God. I learned of the great prophets of old and of my friend, Jesus, as well.

After my initial profession and a certain number of conferences with my pastor in which I disclosed the fact I already knew of my connection to God, which I recounted earlier, I solidified my public profession of Christ with a baptism. My baptism stamped confirmation on the flood with which God had taken hold of my life. I was in love and now everyone knew it. But with my prayers came the call, and with the call I seemed to be pulled in opposite directions with no other recourse than to cry.

Such tears are only beneficial for so long. Unfortunately, I did not know or understand the effects of self-pity and wallowing as I do now. My ignorance led me down a gradual path of resentment and distancing. Those early days of my walk with Him were wonderful despite my gradual separation. I have the fondest memories of the purest kind of relationship with Him. I do not know if time has painted these pictures better than they were, however I do know they were wonderful, and that wonder draws me back to Him daily.

CHAPTER TWO

The All-American Boy

§

When they arrived, Samuel saw Eliab and thought, "Surely the Lord's anointed stands here before the Lord." But the Lord said to Samuel, "Do not consider his appearance or his height, for I have rejected him. The Lord does not look at the things man looks at. Man looks at the outward appearance, but the Lord looks at the heart."
-1 Samuel 16:6-7

Has anyone been in a small-town American high school lately? High schools are dangerous places filled with hopes and dreams, headaches and nightmares, true loves and true disasters. High schools are places in which the raising of children comes to a culmination at the apex of parental supervision and education. It is the place where at 15 years of age, one enters into a world of searching. Searching is something we all must do, but at 15, standing in front of my high school, it seemed like a job a 15-year-old is not capable of doing. How, in this mess of so many people and hormones, was I supposed to find who I was?

I was supposed to find who I was in high school, right? I had the freedom to move without always having my parents by my side, or at least I thought I did. I could go to the restaurants I wanted to go to and eat lunch without my parents even knowing to which restaurant I went. I could play the sports I want to play or join the groups I wanted to join. I had a chance to start all over on the "cool ladder" with all the older students who had been around longer. I had the chance to stand out from all these other people so the world would know who I was.

It seemed, in this exciting adventure of realizing my own identity, the real desire of my heart was always to show the world who I really was. Although not yet formed, my dream was to make my impact on the world with as loud a bang as I could possibly muster. I was going to use all the ability I had been given to make the biggest impact on the biggest stage. What the biggest stage was at age 15 was not something I knew consciously, but subconsciously, I knew very well what that stage was. Subconsciously, the safest course of action was to become an "actor" who was going to win a proverbial Oscar for the role of the "All-American Boy."

Now in case anyone has forgotten, let me explain who the "All-American Boy" is. Everyone has watched him on television, but the sad part is many young men in the real world are convinced these fictional characters are fit role models to try to emulate, and I was certainly no exception. The "All-American Boy' is the kid who excels in everything society expects a good "Red State" boy to excel. The "All-American Boy" is the great athlete. He is not just good at one sport, but he is an overall athlete who dominates all the sports he desires to play and the public desires to watch him play.

He is the boy who all the kids cheer for at the peprallies. He is the boy who won the intramural race in elementary school, and all the kids stood up to cheer for him as he crossed the finish line. Now in high school, he is the same boy who gets his picture in the paper every week for all his athletic accomplishments. The sound of the crowd is his desire. To hear the thousands of people who follow high school sports cheer him on as he scores the winning touchdown or sinks the winning shot. The "All-American Boy" dreams of being talked about at Dairy Queens as he grows up.

Now if one is from small town, Middle America, one knows exactly what I am talking about, but if one is not, let me explain. Dairy Queens, in small towns, are the think tanks of who will be the next local celebrity. It is around pots of coffee in these small restaurants the legends of small-town heroes are made. The next great quarterback or politician will be discussed in these local Dairy Queens. It is in the reminiscing of old men the future dreams of young men see the start of their prominence in the hearts of our society. These old men, who gather every morning for coffee, know every detail of the lives of the up-and-coming high school elite, and they know no greater pleasure than to discuss the future of the pride of their small town.

The "All-American Boy" hopes in attaining this fame, prosperity in the pursuit of female luxury will occur. Female luxury is the after-effect of a "glorious" deposit in the bank of prestige. Female luxury is the overflow of female attention that ensues with the rank of "All-American Boy." It is labeled "luxury" because it does not require any work on the part of the young man; instead, it is the luxury of lying back as the women come to him. This "luxury" is the desire of many entering high school freshmen and most definitely the goal of the "All-American Boy."

The "All-American Boy" hopes to attain this luxury in other ways besides just prestige through sports. It is in appearance the "All-American Boy" also makes his statement. He must be the best-looking guy on campus. He must have the right physique, which should be attained through whatever means necessary. These means will include steroids, or whatever other performance-enhancing drugs are available. I have watched young men in their prime pump themselves full of steroids just for the purpose of looking good. Simply take a stroll down to the nearest State college and enter the campus weight room.

In this weight room, fraternity brothers lifting weights with bodybuilder-like work ethic will be found. I once wondered what exactly these guys were doing, working out so hard, and then I realized exactly what they were doing. With each lift, they stared harder and harder into the mirror. These guys had huge upper bodies and tiny legs, which at the time I found very odd. Then the purpose was very clear to me– they wanted that look of athletic accomplishment. The tiny legs and the huge arms were a sign of the lengths they would go to in order to attain an athletic look. Young men so eager to find acceptance in society, seeking out friendship in fraternities, had injected their body with steroids. Steroid use is the extreme result of finding the right physique, but unfortunately not a rare result. In order to appear to have a great body, all these young men were willing to compromise a healthy body. Somewhere in the warped pursuit of acceptance the *appearance* of health became more important than actual health.

The physique is not the only component of appearance that is important, there must also be the right hair and clothing. Now, no expense should be spared on this important part of the image. Only the most in-style and expensive clothing can be included in the wardrobe of the "All-American Boy." Whatever his parents will let him buy, that is what he spends when trying to obtain the proper image. I have seen people spend one hundred fifty dollars on tennis shoes to try and achieve the proper appearance. What does it say about the "All-American Boy" that he feels a need to spend one hundred fifty dollars on tennis shoes? If I am not mistaken, these one hundred fifty dollar tennis shoes are really no different in functionality than the twenty dollar tennis shoes at the local Wal-Mart, but people pay one hundred fifty dollars because the name of the most popular basketball player is on the shoe. One hundred fifty dollars, so other people *might* associate him with a certain famous basketball player.

CHAPTER THREE

The All-American Boy Never Bucks the Popular Crowd

§

A champion named Goliath, who was from Gath, came out of the Philistine camp. He was over nine feet tall. He had a bronze helmet on his head and wore a coat of scale armor of bronze weighing five thousand shekels; on his legs he wore bronze greaves, and a bronze javelin was slung on his back.
-1 Samuel 17:4-6

Around three thousand years ago, in the desert that is our Holy Land, a battle was fought by a young man. This battle was to represent his whole country and the future of his people. A young man stepped out that day and raised his voice when all those around him were running away. This young man who was to be a king stepped out and faced a monster when all those around him were mocking him for his courage. This young man spoke up and announced the presence of God among his people was enough to over- come the power of their enemies. This young man stood in front of a giant who mocked all that his people held as good and true. This giant mocked the God of this young man's people, their king, and the people themselves, and so the young man stood up and fought. Young King David showed us three thousand years ago what a son of God should act like, but after three thousand years, what do we aspire to be as young men?

The "All-American Boy" does not desire to step out and be mocked by the soldiers of his time. It does not matter if principles are in question, what really matters is the appearance of the young man among his peers. Unlike King David, the "All-American Boy" tries to avoid upsetting the popular crowd, or the crowd who gives him popularity, at all costs. The crowd is who gives us our worth in modern times. It is not derived from some higher authority, but it is found in the applause of the arena, the flash of photography, and the writing of the newspaper. It is in these media outlets the "All-American Boy" seeks to find his worth and value.

The days of esteeming priests and monks are long gone and so is the young man's desire to be valued for the reasons priests and monks were once valued. It is not the desire of the "All-American Boy" to be valued because he fears God, but to find favor in the crowd by submitting to the fear of standing against them. In sharing the details of my life, it is my intention to show how easy it is to deviate from God's plan for us.

I personally know this principle of the "All-American Boy" all too well. It is interesting how the events of one's ignorant youth come back to haunt him. I am haunted by the things I have done in the past and at the same time, I am grateful for the lessons God has begun to teach me through them. In my pursuit of being the "All-American Boy," I refused to stand up against the crowd. Call it peer pressure, or whatever, but I was still at fault, no matter what it is called. I knew what was right and what was not, and I did not stand up. Faced with the opportunity to fear God more than men, faced with the opportunity to make a stand for Christianity, I feared the crowd more than I believed God.

I was in eighth grade the day we had a free day as the B-team practiced for an upcoming basketball game. We were in our small junior high gym that afternoon. It was one of those gyms that was really barely a gym. It was not full-sized and the roof was too low to really play. I remember shooting so many shots at that goal and so many hitting the rafters that hung over the court at a level that was just right for blocking a long arching shot. The gym was dim and not very appealing to the eye. It was made out of cinderblocks painted a nasty green in some old attempt at school spirit.

This was the typical junior high gym in a small town. It had stands, but the stands were only on one side of the gym and they were the small, aluminum stands one can move just by pushing. As the B-team was going through their practice, I was sitting in the top of the aluminum stands talking about all the silly things junior high boys talk about. As I sat there talking with my friends, in what would be considered the cool group, there was a disruption under the stands.

A couple of guys had engaged in some under-the-stands fighting. As is the custom in junior high, everyone got very excited and began to cheer and yell. As I become more aware of what was going on, I realized who it was doing the fighting. If I was in the cool group that day, the young man fighting was definitely not. I do not recall the other guy in the fight, I just remember Bubba.

Bubba was one of those kids most people only see in movies. Bubba was a kid who was slower than everyone else. He was not mentally retarded, but he was very much on the slow side, as was demonstrated by his appearance. Bubba was one of those kids who acted out, and when he did, it was aggravating, but somewhere deep inside I could not really blame him for his actions. Bubba was not just slow, he was the epitome of a kid from a dysfunctional family.

When we were in third grade, Bubba was in my class as well. One day while we were in class, there was a big uproar out in the hall. Our classroom was right across from the principal's office, and there was a woman out in the hall screaming. I was young and I do not remember exactly what was being said, but I remember the main point. Bubba's mom had come up to the school and was threatening to do something awful to the school if she did not get whatever it was she wanted. From that time on, I knew Bubba's life was a lot different than mine.

See, Bubba's mom was one of those women who looked past middle age, even though she was not that old. Life had been hard on this woman and it was apparent. She had very long, unkempt, brown hair mixed with gray that had come before its time. She was wrinkled well beyond her years and her teeth were of such a poor quality it made me draw back a bit. This poor lady was one of those people who was most likely a little off her rocker, and poor Bubba bore the results of growing up in this situation.

Now this day in the gym, Bubba was acting out, and as I look back, I cannot really blame him. I am not saying getting in a fist fight is ever justified, but I can look back now and have so much more sympathy for the condition of this young man. As the fight was broken up, the crowd around was called into action by the coach who was responsible for watching this huge group of junior high boys.

In response to the fight, the coach decided to instill in us a sense of teamwork and self-discipline. Coach was burdened that day with trying to keep us in line and trying to coach the B-team for their upcoming game at the same time. In order to try and accomplish all this, we were given the responsibility of administering Bubba's punishment for initiating the fist fight.

In traditional athletic fashion, Bubba was given the punishment of doing push-ups. This was not a particularly hard punishment, but for Bubba that day, it was bad enough. As we all circled up to make sure Bubba would do his push-ups, Bubba refused. Bubba refusing to do his push-ups would not have been that big of a deal if it had not been for Coach's edict that if Bubba did not do his push-ups, we would all be responsible and the punishment would be worse.

The fear of having to exert ourselves for Bubba's misdoings was too much for a bunch of junior high boys, so all fifty of us were urging Bubba to do his push-ups. Despite all of our efforts, Bubba refused. Now as a leader in almost all our sports, and as the potential "All-American Boy" even then, I decided it was my job to make sure Bubba did his push-ups. At first, I urged him like everyone else, but when my encouragement did not work, I got frustrated. I decided I would try to help Bubba by using my own strength and told him I would do the push-ups with him. I got down and began to do push-ups. When I got down Bubba got up and said, "You can do them, because I am not going to."

I was starting to look bad in front of everyone else and I was getting mad at Bubba for not doing what I saw as a very remedial punishment for his transgression. I am not sure what my motivation was, but I jumped up and began to yell at Bubba. I told him with a very passionate scolding he was going to do those push-ups, one way or another. As I did this, I grabbed Bubba by the shirt and swept his legs out from under him. I did this because I wanted to get Bubba back on the ground doing his push-ups, and for some reason I thought this would accomplish that most effectively. Bubba fell hard on the ground, but all my effort did was make him more determined to stand back up.

I do not think I realized what would happen at the time, but my actions had an effect on the guys around me, too, and not just on Bubba. After I swept his feet out from under him, Bubba stood back up and began to shout at everyone that he was not going to do his push-ups. As Bubba began to shout, one of the young men standing beside me jumped out and slugged Bubba right in the face. Bubba's poor round frame, much fluffier and shorter than anyone else there, fell to the ground. This was not just a love tap, and it bloodied Bubba's face and caused him to cry quite a lot.

Bubba never finished his push-ups. The new fight was broken up by Coach and we were all sent back into the gym. As I sit here and think about that day, in eighth grade, I feel great pain. I feel pain for Bubba and I feel pain I was so obsessed with attaining the image I thought I wanted that I was capable of doing something so horrible to someone so young and vulnerable. Why did not I just do the push-ups for Bubba?

I wish I could say after eight grade and Bubba, I changed my view of what was expected of me when it came to standing up to the crowd, but I did not. One would think I would learn from my experiences, but many times I have not and still do not. Just one year later, life gave me the chance to stand up against the crowd again.

Freshmen in high school endure a lot. There is the anxiety of starting a school where most of the people are a lot bigger and more experienced with life. Any time it is the first year at the bottom of the food chain it is a hard time, and one's freshman year of high school is no different. Add on the changes in hormones and all the bodily fluctuations that go with that time of life, and it is incredibly awkward and difficult. My experience as a freshman was the same and no less scary.

When I was a freshman, we had a sharp dichotomy in our athletic department. Athletics were life to me and to my school, so this dichotomy was very much a part of my life and I was very aware of it. The dichotomy consisted of those who played football and those who did not. Football was the sport in my small town, so the group who did not play was basically a small group of outcasts who were stuck in a small locker room by themselves. These outcasts were not given great supervision because the number of football players was so great that much of the coaching resources we had were required to deal with the football teams. Every day during our athletic period, the football players would get dressed in the main locker rooms while the off-season outcasts would get dressed in their small locker room off to the side.

There were no coaches in the small locker room while the boys got dressed because their off-season coach was a woman. The boys in-season my freshman year were an interesting group. They consisted of varying guys ranging from the older "stud" baseball players to the very young freshmen, who were more interested in the social aspects of sports than they were in actually being athletic as they were still very skinny. The older boys looked more like the actors who play high school kids in the movies than they did like actual high school kids. These older guys were the guys in high school who had to shave every morning or they would have a beard by the afternoon. These older guys were a wild bunch, and had been as long as I had known them, but wild, older-looking, and talented was what was cool in high school, and as freshmen we were all very aware of this fact. These guys were everything we were not.

I was not in the off-season locker room my freshman year, but I heard about what went on and so did everyone else. I, like everyone else, did not make a big stand or say anything about the older guys' actions toward these guys. Not only did I not say anything about their actions, but I laughed at what they did. I laughed as people were humiliated. That year while I was getting dressed in the main locker room, the outcast locker room was experiencing persecution. This persecution was the result of what happens when society tells young men the image they need to project is a wild, untamed, macho, and abusive one. The older boys decided they needed to improve their images as the macho athletes by preying on those younger than themselves in that outcast locker room.

There were two young freshmen in the outcast locker room and both were my friends. They were not my best friends, but they were friends, nonetheless. These two freshmen, Harry and Carl, were both kids who were not yet fully matured. They were kids who were a lot smaller than even people their own age, and a whole lot smaller than these older guys. One day, as they got dressed to go to the off-season workout, the older boys decided to do some hazing. As Harry got dressed, they grabbed him and held him down on the ground. Harry tried to fight, but he was much smaller than just one of the guys, much less multiple guys. So Harry struggled to no avail. As they held him down, one of the older guys pulled out his genitalia and stuck it in Harry's ear. As Harry struggled and tried to fight back, the older student rubbed himself all over Harry's face, taunting him and mocking him.

No one fought for Harry. After they were done with Harry, they decided they were not finished and they grabbed Carl. They held Carl down and no one stopped them. After they had pinned Carl to the ground, one of the older guys took off his pants and his underwear and proceeded to sit on Carl's face. This was not done in prison or in a juvenile detention center, but in the high school of a small town in Middle America. No one stopped them in that room and the dissent in the room, which was present, was held to a hush. I do not sit in judgment on the people in that room who did not speak up and I do not sit in judgment on the guys who did this deed. See, later on I laughed at this very thing and I did not stand up and condemn it when it was talked about around school. Actions were taken by parents, but I was not a voice of challenge. I was not a voice of opposition to the cool kids.

I have to ask myself why I acted the way I acted. As I thought about it later in life, I discovered something about myself and about those involved. We all acted out of fear. The kids who did this awful thing did so because they feared if they did not portray the image of the strong jock, they might not get the acceptance they needed. They felt by doing this awful deed they would be able to build upon the image they were trying to achieve. They believed this image was acceptable or something to be desired, and those with power should exhibit that power over those who were weaker. In domination of something weaker they themselves would be shown to be strong.

I do not totally fault them for this, because the world they grew up in values this principle. We honor those with power in our society. We invite the principal of the high school to a banquet, but not the janitor. We want the doctors and lawyers to marry our sons and daughters, but not the postal workers or waiters. When was the last time a parent was heard to say he or she hopes his or her child marries a postal worker? Why is that? Postal workers are good people doing a good job our country relies on to run. The reason is postal workers are not perceived as powerful. Money and power are synonymous in our capitalistic society and postal workers do not have large amounts of money. Parents value power and money and they want that perceived security for their children.

Now, with these shortcomings in mind, these guys who did this awful thing to Carl and Harry simply wanted what every parent in the United States seems to express to want for their child: power. The difference is these guys were in high school and could not make large amounts of money. So the place in which they found what society told them they needed was in the torturing of poor freshmen boys. I am not excusing their actions by any means, I am simply asking the question: Why did they do it?

The people who did not say anything in the locker room while these acts were happening to Carl and Harry were also motivated by fear. It was the same fear that motivated me. It was the fear of opposing the popular group. In a world where image is acceptance, having one's image tarnished in the eyes of the popular group is to lose one's worth in the eyes of the world. The image back then we all had worked so hard to create, all of us at different levels of success, but all of us working hard to get where we were, did not want to lose that status by opposing the crowd. I laughed because others laughed. I did not speak out against it because others saw it as something that should not be spoken out against. Those in the off-season locker room did not speak out against it because they did not want to be next and because they wanted to be cool, too.

This is the life in which we live, a life where actions are not driven by right and wrong, but by acceptance in the eyes of those who have taken power. We live in a time when people run from Goliaths. We run from those who would mock our beliefs and would take our lives by force. It is not whether something is of good merit, it is whether that something will benefit us or not. In corporate America, it is not whether the jobs we create in third-world countries are good for the people in third-world countries, it is whether or not those jobs are low-paying enough to profit our companies. In high school, it is not whether we should stand up for those in need, our friends in need, it is whether standing up will make us more popular with the in-crowd or not.

The days are now, when we are in need of a David. We are in need of men who will stand up in the face of mocking and great adversity and stand for the merit God sees, not the merit man pursues. Now are the days for the changing of thoughts to honor, not to those with perceived power, but to those worth honoring. It is time we as a society honored the "Davids" among us and applauded the slaying of "Goliaths."

CHAPTER FOUR

The All-American Boy Always Performs

§

Goliath stood and shouted to the ranks of Israel, "Why do you come out and line up for battle? Am I not a Philistine, and are you not the servants of Saul? Choose a man and have him come down to me. If he is able to fight and kill me, we will become your subjects; but if I overcome him and kill him, you will become our subjects and serve us. -1 Samuel 17:8-9

"We want, we want, we want the Gobblers! We want, we want, we want the Gobblers!" The tunnel was dark and enormous as the crowd called for our team, but the feeling of being stacked in line, in between my teammates, was one that brought familiarity. The tunnel, however, was not something that felt familiar in any way. It was big! Not just in size, although the size of the tunnel was intimidating, but the tunnel was big in atmosphere. The atmosphere of that tunnel was one that cannot be explained unless a person has felt it himself. It is a feeling of pressure, a feeling of responsibility, the pressure and responsibility of thousands of people on one's shoulders. It is the feeling that comes as a 16-year-old waits in the tunnel of the Astrodome in Houston, Texas to play his first State Championship as the starting quarterback.

It had not been an easy path to that tunnel, and all the emotions and scares created along the way made the weightiness of that tunnel seem all the heavier. Our team had been through a lot, and so had I. We started off the year with high expectations because Cuero, Texas always has high expectations for football, but no one thought we would take those expectations to the State Championship. The thought of being in the State Championship was even less likely with me a quarterback because I started the year as a back-up. I was a back-up who was talked about, but I was a back-up, nonetheless.

The first few games of that year I played end, guard, and tackle: I sat on the end of the bench, guarded the water bottle, and tackled anyone who came near it. Okay, I did not really tackle anyone, but I was a quarterback, cut me some slack. Now, it sounds like I just sat on the sidelines, content to be on varsity and watch our team play, but that was not the case at all. I was unhappy and I did not try to hide it one bit. As I look back, I wonder why I was so discontent. I was a sophomore on varsity and the second-string quarterback who was thought well of by many people in my town. There was no real reason to be unhappy with my situation, if it was not for expectations.

Remember, I was playing the part of the "All-American Boy" and there are certain expectations that come with that role. I had to be the best if everyone was going to think of me the way I thought they should. The best is not second-string and I knew that, so I had to be the best! There is a movie which illustrates my point pretty well, although I hesitate to use movie analogies because everyone may not have seen this particular one. This movie in particular is not one I recommend, but it hits so close to home I cannot help but use it to illustrate.

Varsity Blues came out when I was in high school and demonstrates the epitome of the "All-American Boy" syndrome. The town portrayed in this movie is the ultimate football town and, unfortunately, parts of it are not a lot different from many of the little football-crazed towns in Texas today. In the movie, there is a kid by the name of John Moxon who is just a second-string quarterback on a great team. This kid is smart and not really all that into football, but his dad loves the game and so he plays for him. In the movie, no one really knows who the back-up quarterback is and no one really cares until the starter blows out his knee and Moxon has to step in and play.

Moxon steps in to the starting quarterback position and his whole life changes. All of the sudden, he is the town celebrity and the old starting quarterback is lost in a blur. The movie goes on to tell a bunch of details about this kid's adventure to find who he is in this newfound situation, but I think the point is clear. This movie was really popular when it came out, and not because people like football so much. People do like football, but the reason they like football and would like a movie about football is much different than some people may think. From the perspective of almost every young "Moxon" in America, people like football because people like winners. People want a hero and if they have to produce one by setting little kids up in pads and seeing who will come out on top, then so be it. People liked *Varsity Blues* because deep down most Americans want to be a "Moxon". People want the town to love them and people want to be on top.

As I sat there on the sidelines, I was unhappy because sidelines are not the place where heroes are made in our society. How many times does one hear a kid at a football game say, "Hey, look at that cool water boy! I sure do want to be a water boy when I grow up"? Those words are never heard in the stands and if they are heard, it is to mock the water boys. What does that say about us? What does it say that we mock water boys, but we praise rappers who use drugs and sing about it?

I was so discontent sitting on the sidelines, without the ability to be in the spot light, I actually asked my offensive coordinator if I could move down to junior varsity. I did not really want to play on junior varsity, but I thought it would give me a chance to show what I could do. Not only that, but I was so concerned with losing my abilities on the sideline and losing my chance to be the hero I was willing to leave my team without a back-up quarterback to go and play on junior varsity.

However, I ended up not having to play on junior varsity, because just a couple of games after I made my request, the starting quarterback broke his arm. I should describe the starting quarterback: He was one of those guys who had mighty potential. "Mighty" was one of those guys who could do anything he wanted, one just never knew what he was going to want. Mighty was a good-looking black guy who was incredibly talented. In fact, Mighty was so talented that after his sophomore year, we went to a Nebraska football camp together and Nebraska was already calling for him by the time we got back to town.

Mighty was one of those players everyone talked about even though he really had not done much on the field. Mighty had a lot of potential, but he came from the "other side" of our small town and no matter where a person grows up, he or she knows what I mean when I say the "other side" of town. Every town has them and has had them for as long as history records. The "other side" of town is the poor part of town, the part of town that is not as safe and not as nice. Now, in south central Texas, that part of town tends to be more highly populated by minority races, and in Cuero it was no different. Because of the differences in race and wealth, although I think it is more wealth than race, there was, and regrettably still is, a strong division in the town between black and white.

So, Mighty broke his arm in the very beginning of the game, and I was thrown into the spotlight. It has been a long time since I played that particular game, but I remember it very well. I had a rough first half playing quarterback: I rolled out to throw a pass and I got clobbered as soon as I turned out of my roll. Then, the ball popped up and the defense caught it and ran the length of the field for a touchdown. We were down at half-time even though we were not supposed to lose to this team. We were playing the Hallettsville Brahmas and we were losing. We were losing, and it was my first game to really play. The fans in the stands were not too hard on me that game, mostly because I think they were still in shock from losing Mighty.

I remember half-time of that game. For some reason we sat outside of the locker room, and I was sitting on my helmet. As I sat there, mostly just trying to catch my breath, Mighty came up to me with his arm in a sling. Mighty slapped me on the back and told me I could do it, although I was not sure if he really believed it as he told me. After Mighty's pep talk, I realized he was not coming back to play with a broken arm and this was my chance. It was my chance to shine and as I sat there I thought to myself, *I* can *do this, and I* will *do this*. After half-time, we went out on the field and we laid it to the Brahmas like never before. My offensive line helped me rack up two hundred fifty yards rushing in the second half and five rushing touchdowns. It was a great game, and the start to a great year.

We actually lost the next game we played and the first game that I ever really started. After that loss, however, we went on to make the playoffs in a very convincing fashion and ended up in the Class 3A Large School bracket of the State Playoffs. As we marched toward the playoffs, my team enjoyed success and so did I. I was racking up yards left and right, I was in the newspaper every week, and the "big" newspaper in Victoria, Texas did a special article all about me. I was in the middle of it. I was in the middle of the All-American Boy's dream. I was the town hero and I was a star. I was only 16 and I was the starting quarterback of the Cuero Gobblers. As I progressed, so did the healing of Mighty's arm, creating the elements for a perfect storm of high school controversy.

It was the playoffs and Mighty was healthy again. The problem was I was playing really well and I was the one who had led the team to the playoffs. The other problem was the family I came from. I was the son of the town doctor and I was white. This caused a crisis that was bigger than who the deserving player was, it was a question of who the deserving person was. Coach had to make a call and looking back, I realize it must have been a very hard call to make. It was not like Mighty was a bad player; Mighty was a guy whom a lot of college coaches were watching. In the end, Coach decided to let me start and let me play quarterback while he moved Mighty to wide receiver. As one can imagine, this went well with half the stands and did not go well with the other half. I was thankful for the decision and I went on and played as hard as I could, and we did well.

We soldiered on through the playoffs, beating all the valley teams in the first few rounds, and progressing all the way to the quarterfinals of the State playoffs. Now in Cuero, the quarterfinals are a big deal because of "the sign." The sign is a big board that sits in front of the high school. The only teams that get their name on the sign are those teams that make it to the State quarterfinals in their sport. The sign was not just a wooden board; it was a signal a person had arrived in Cuero athletics. The night we won the quarterfinal game I was so excited and as I sat in the locker room, I could not help but take it all in. The music was blaring from the jukebox the guys had brought. Everyone was dancing and yelling, it was like something out of a movie and I was so happy. That night was really the last time I was euphoric about football.

Our next game was against Giddings, and we were playing at the Alamodome in San Antonio. I remember the bus ride up to that game was full of pressure, but not all that heavy for some reason. The semifinals are a place of status, and as a sophomore I felt like that honor was enough for me. I felt as a team we had done well and I was happy with our performance. I thought we could win, and that thought helped to alleviate a lot of the pressure. Although the pressure was not really affecting me adversely, the strength of the other team ended up causing a lot of problems I did not anticipate.

As it turned out, Giddings was good. Playing in the Alamodome had invigorated our whole team. San Antonio was not far from home and the stadium was really new which meant all the facilities were incredible nice. It was the first real dome our team had played in that year and when one is a teenager, that distinction is exciting. We ran all over that field before game time talking about how we were walking in the same place the San Antonio Spurs would play.

Yet thinking of playing on the same ground as professional athletes did not help us much, as Giddings was beating us at the half. Giddings, by all accounts, should have beaten us that game; they were everywhere on that field. On offense, Giddings pounded away at us with a big tailback who just kept plugging yard after yard down the field. It seemed like every play we ran was overwhelmed by Giddings defensive players. I was hit in the back on the third step of my three-step drop, and when we would run the option, I would be hit in the mouth by the defensive end and our tailback would find the same results, except with the linebackers.

We were down by two touchdowns in the second half when the tide started to turn. The coaches took me to the side and told me we were going to improvise on offense. We were going to run a bootleg to the left side of the field and alter the tight end's route so he was running toward the right corner of the field. This was going to be a difficult throw for me to make because I would have to throw back across the field to the opposite side of the one to which I was running. We ran out onto the field after my conversation with the coach and ran the bootleg.

Now, I should have been terrified at the thought of running such a risky play at a key moment in the game, but when I was playing I never thought about what could happen if I messed up. So I took the snap and rolled toward the left hash. As I set up in the pocket I looked back for my tight end and saw him make his cut. As he planted his foot in the ground to break toward the opposite corner, I let the ball fly. Right after I let the ball go, a knot rose up in my throat. I watch helplessly as my tight end fell right over his own feet as he came out of his cut. The ball was flying through the air and my intended receiver was on lying on his face. As I panicked, watching my receiver fall, one of my best friends on the team was running a backside post from the far right receiver position. Sean saw the ball in the air and adjusted his route to take off after it. Thirty-five yards down the field, Sean pulled off the biggest catch of the season as he dove to catch my pass that was intended for the tight end.

It is interesting how the things we intend are not always the things that are best for us. All I thought about was the route we altered in the pattern, and I had forgotten the backside receiver's route would cross right in front of the adjusted route. In the middle of a giant disaster, my mistake gave my friend an opportunity to be great. Sean's catch was the best part of that game. After Sean's catch, we scored a touchdown and pulled within a score. Our defense made a huge play by intercepting a pass, and for the first time the momentum of the game was in our favor. We capitalized on the momentum by completing a big pass to Mighty and then some key runs to put us on the goal line.

We ran a quarterback sneak three times before I was finally able to stand behind my offensive line and stretch the ball over for the score. We took the lead with that touchdown and the excitement of the comeback slowed as I ran off the field knowing we had won the game. I had run the ball almost thirty times that game and had taken a number of blows. It was as if I was in some sort of athletic trance up until that final touchdown, and after the score I began to come back to my body. As started to feel more grounded, I realized I was not exactly myself and my knee was killing me. Once I got to the sidelines, I sat down and had the trainers take a look at my leg.

What they found was something I did not want to see. My knee was swollen so large they could not get my pants up high enough to look at it. As I sat there, the normal emotion of fear did not overwhelm me like I thought it should have. Instead, they cut my pants to take a closer look at my knee and I stared out at the game, knowing we were going to State. My team, the team I quarterbacked, was going to State. The last Cuero quarterback to take a team to State played for the Nebraska

Cornhuskers in a National Championship game. This semifinal win was my arrival, and as I sat there on the sidelines I thought all I had wanted had finally come.

After the game, I did not enjoy the celebration as I did after our quarterfinal win because I went straight to the training room where they began to work on my knee. My knee was not in good shape, and the full understanding of how bad it was tempered my excitement about our win. I began to realize in the locker room that in a very short time, I was going to have to play a State Championship game and I could hardly walk. My father is a doctor, and he came in and looked at my knee that night and assured me it was just a burst of a sack in my knee and the fluid would soon go away.

His assurance was good, but the uncertainty of my leg caused me to be reserved in my celebration of our victory. As we all have a tendency to do, I was so concerned with a future I could not control that I missed the blessing I had been given in the present. So I trooped through the next week with enthusiasm, but with a cloud of concern hanging over my head. I rested my knee all week until finally, with just a few days until game time, I had to take action to ensure I would be able to play. My knee was still enormous, and I could not run with all the fluid built up in my joint, so I went down to my father's office and I laid there as he drained two really large syringes of blood and fluid off my knee.

After the encounter with the really big needles, which I hated, I was able to walk and run. My knee was weak, but it was functional, and a weak knee was not going to stop me from playing in the State Championship. After all, my image was at stake. My success as a quarterback was at stake, and Mighty was sitting right behind me to take my place. I was not about to let Mighty step in and take all the glory I had dreamed about my whole life. It dawned on me that although I was content with our success in the semifinals, other people were not going to be as gracious if I was not to play. I began to feel the pressure build as the day of the State game grew closer and my knee remained weak.

If a person did not grow up in a town that lives and breathes football, then it will be hard for him or her to understand the atmosphere that week in Cuero. It was like a holiday in the middle of the year. I do not remember doing any real school work and there was decoration everywhere. The cheerleaders had decorated the halls all over the school, but they did not stop there. The whole town was decorated for the game. The windows of the banks and restaurants were all decorated with window chalk and every street I walked down was covered with some sort of decoration. The cheerleaders even decorated my *room*.

The week was truly wonderful, but for someone who felt the weight of the game on their back, all the decorations and celebration just seemed to increase the pressure. It was as if with every cheer and decoration given, even though in good intention, the expectations grew greater. The week's celebrations were capped off with a parade. As we pulled out on our buses that Saturday morning, we were greeted with a parade around town led by police and firemen. It seemed like the whole town was out on the street to wish us good luck. These were our parents and friends, but they were also the people of Cuero.

The people of Cuero are known for football. If someone says he or she is from Cuero, people will only know where it is because he or she lives where the Cuero Gobblers play football. It was as if all those people were depending on us to hold up their identity in some way. The town was out to wish us good luck, to show us support, and to show us how much they cared about our game. They cared about our game enough to throw us a parade and I was the one responsible for the ball on offense. I was the quarterback. I was the one they looked to for success. After the parade, we set off for Houston and the State game.

"We want, we want, we want the Gobblers!" The tunnel was big in the Astrodome that day, because the State game held all the expectations of my town and my life. As I ran out of the tunnel that Saturday, I met all the expectations and fears head on as I led my team against the Aledo Bearcats. I ran out onto the field and began to think of the well-arranged game plan that had been laid out to beat Aledo. We were going to run our usual offense with a few new bootlegs to get me out in the open. I began to think of what I needed to do to win. As I thought, new pressures arose in my mind. Right before the game, we were watching Judson, a large 5A school, play for the State Championship, and as we sat there, one of the players from a previous State Championship team came up to me and started to give me advice.

He had good intentions, but as he lectured me on how to throw the ball and not to overthrow my receivers at the beginning of the game, I began to feel like I was young and inadequate. This man's face was popping in my head as I ran out onto the field, and the thought of so many people watching me was overwhelming. Because of the 5A game that preceded our game, there were more people in the stands than I had ever played in front of. The lower section of the stadium was almost completely full and I knew there were college scouts sitting in those seats. Despite my fears and all the people, I went out and led our offense.

The first drive was impressive. We ran our new bootlegs and they were working beautifully. We would run a counter trap with the tailback and then we would run a bootleg, and it was marching us down the field. The second time we ran the bootleg, I busted out into the secondary and took off. I felt myself pulling away and the excitement that comes with pulling away rushed through me until *BOOM*, someone hit me from my blind side. It was the safety and he hit me hard. I flew up into the air and landed on my head. The Astrodome was not nearly as nice as the Alamodome because it had been a few years since the Houston Oilers were in Houston and the facilities were old. The Astroturf I landed on was not very forgiving and as my head impacted the ground, I was knocked unconscious. I laid on the ground for just a few seconds until my teammates came down the field and picked me up. I was woozy, but I got up and headed back to the huddle.

One might wonder why I did not come out of the game after a hit that knocked me out, and to answer that question, one must remember the feeling I had as I realized I might not be able to play in the State game. I was not about to let Mighty come in when I had just taken the ball all the way down the field. So we were on about the 20-yard line, I had to score, and we drove the ball all the way down to the 2- or 3-yard line before it was fourth and goal. On fourth down, we went for it and the ball was put in my hands. Right before the play started, our head coached looked at me and said, "Andrew, if you can run it in, run it in, and only throw it if you have to."

Those words rang through my mind as I came to the line. We were running the bootleg again and it was up to me to put it in the end zone. I took the snap and sprinted out to the left, and as I came around the corner, I took off as fast as I could to get around end. I made it around end and only the cornerback and I remained. The cornerback was guarding Mighty in the end zone and as I turned up field, all that came into my head was, "Run it if you can," so that is just what I did. When the cornerback saw I was going to run, he stopped guarding Mighty and came up to make a play on me. On the one yard line, we collided and I was stopped short of a touchdown.

The first drive of my first state game was prophetic, to say the least. I came so close and yet came up just short of my intended goal. The first drive ended and we did not score. We would not score until well into the second half, but our opponents put up 13 points in the second half. We were down 13 to 0 when I finally threw a touchdown pass to the same friend who had saved me in the semifinal game. It was the fourth quarter and we were down by 6 points when we got the ball back with just a few minutes left in the game.

The end of important close games seems like it should be nerve-racking, but when one is in the middle of the fight, it is never as it appears to the spectators. As I took the field I was not aware of how nervous I should be, I only seemed to be aware of the task in front of me. We had great field position and we went straight to our bread-and-butter bootleg play. I got under center and rolled out to the left side of the field. We called a bootleg throwback in the huddle, and as I rolled left, my tailback was running down the right side of the field. I did not even think about what to do. I knew Bebe, my running back, would be there and I let it rip. The ball flew down the field and landed right in Bebe's arms. We were on the 25-yard line with enough time to score and a chance to win the game.

The next play from scrimmage was an option pass, and as I went down the line, I decided to look straight to my outside receiver, even though my first read was my inside receiver. I watched as one of my best friends planted his toe in the ground and looked for the ball and as he did, I threw an awful pass that flew right by him. What I did not notice, but everyone in the stands certainly did, was that Mighty, who was playing inside receiver, was wide open running down the field. My inability to find Mighty on the route was nothing conscious, but was simply a lapse in judgment on my read. Despite having no intention to mess up, my lapse in judgment would cost me in public opinion. Missing Mighty down the middle was not to be my largest blunder.

With time running down, the intensity with which everyone felt the need to score was growing, and I could feel it as well. I went back to the huddle and waited to receive the play from Coach. Coach decided to choose the play that had been working well for us all night. As I approached the line, both the defense and I were concentrating on the same thing: We both knew I was going to run a bootleg pass and we were both thinking about how to capitalize off of it. I took the snap and faked the hand off, and as I turned out of my fake, I saw the very thing I did not want to see. There were two defensive players already in the backfield and I had nowhere to go.

Sensing I must do something, I tried to turn the other direction in hopes of escaping long enough to get a pass off. This was fourth down, and I knew if I did not escape, the ball was going to be turned over without enough time to get it back. I ran as hard as I could, but on that night it was not enough, and I was sacked in the backfield for a loss. As I got up and headed back for the sidelines, I was not completely aware of what had happened. I soon was made aware, however, as one of my teammates grabbed me and began to yell, "Throw the f—ing ball." His comments would sting for longer than he could possibly know. I had not meant to get sacked or to miss a receiver downfield. It was not my intention to lose the game, but by the accounts of many around me, I had done exactly that.

The game ended with us losing to a team that was not as good as we were, though not a bad team. We got on the bus and headed home with the loss weighing very heavily on our hearts. Everyone expected us to win and we had let them down and the pain of letting the town and our friends down was a very heavy burden for such a young group of men. I was grieving, but my grief was overcome by the effects of my head injury I had suffered early in the game. We stopped to eat on the way home, but instead of eating I threw up most of the time the bus was stopped. It seems that after great losses, vomit comes as the scarlet patch to those whose pride has been squelched.

I would spend the better part of the next day in bed trying to recover from the physical and emotional blows which had been dealt the night before. I got up feeling better and ready to face the world again. It is interesting how God allows us to only know that which we need to know in order to continue on the path we must walk. If I had known what lay ahead of me, I am not sure I would have risen to face the world as I did.

CHAPTER FIVE

An Unforgiving World

§

David left his things with the keeper of the supplies, ran to the battle lines, and greeted his brothers. As he was talking with them, Goliath, the Philistine champion from Gath, stepped out from his lines and shouted his usual defiance, and David heard it. -1 Samuel 17:22-23

I have learned the power of words in my short life. Words can give hope and life to those who no longer have it. Words can inspire people to build the pyramids and others to paint the Mona Lisa. I am afraid most of us know words can also cause great pain and even death. The death words bring can stretch from Nazi genocide to the death of the hopes of a young child. Words can bring the death of a beautiful young woman's self-esteem and the destruction of a young man's courage.

I know both sides of the coin when it comes to words. After the loss of the State Championship, I began to feel the hurt words can cause in a whole new way. A few words from a few people can color a whole group in the thoughts of those that hear them. After I performed below the expectations of most people, my reception was less than cordial. From my vantage point now, I believe this to be because of the loud response of a few and not because of an overall consensus of opinion. I must admit, though, at the time, this fact was not apparent to me. What was apparent then were the actions taken against me by some.

Not long after coming back to school, I was greeted in our parking lot by a note. My car was parked toward the back of the lot near the administration buildings, facing the road on which most people drove down to pick up and drop off kids. To say the least, the position of my car was very much accessible to the public. As I walked out to my car after class, I began to notice writing on my windows. It was written in the green window chalk the cheerleaders used to decorate the town. My first thought was that someone was being funny and had left cute remarks all over my car, as is often seen on kid's cars in high school parking lots. As I walked closer, I saw there was nothing cute about the remarks.

Written all over my car were expletives proceeded by my football number. To this day, I do not know who wrote on my car because I was too embarrassed to ask around school. I am sure there were many people who were not happy with me and many people who may have been tempted to do it, but it should be known I harbor no resentment toward the person or people who wrote it. I only bring it up to show how much words can hurt when used improperly. I am not sure if at that point in my life anything hurt my pride so much.

I was already stung by the loss of the game and the guilt of not playing well. I felt deeply the town's pride and the hopes others had in our victory. I did not need to be told I was not good in such a vehement way. After the incident was done, I wiped off the marker so no one could see it and as I did, I wiped away a piece of my heart I had unconsciously reserved for people of the town.

One would think my experience in that parking lot would have affected the way I felt about football, but it really just fueled the same desire. My love for football did not diminish with the words on my windshield, but my drive to spite the world through success grew with every move of the windshield wiper.

Attitudes in life are usually built over time and develop into the full grown paradigms adults harbor. My feeling toward the public in general also moved in this fashion. I did not form total resentment of the public with this one incident, but the fire was started in my heart and I did not have the wisdom to squelch it myself. Instead, I was content to harbor the fire while others fueled it in me.

The attacks on me did not stop with car chalking, but continued in both private and public sectors. I am not sure which hurt worse, the malicious comments of the people I thought to be friends, or the public comments of those people to whom I had no real attachment. The public attacks I will only show in brevity, for it is not my intention to dwell on such things for long. I find it bad for my soul, even as I write this, to dwell on things of this nature for long periods.

Our town had and still has a movie shop. Most small towns have a store which is taking the place of a local Blockbuster video and ours was the movie shop. I am an avid movie buff, as is most of my family, and we spent a lot of time and money at our local video store. We were frequent customers there, and one night I decided to go and rent a movie. As I stood there in line, a woman was in front of me. I am not sure exactly who she was, although I had seen her around town in the past. I do not know if she knew who I was, but in our small town I find it unlikely she did not know my face. Regardless of whether or not she knew me, what transpired is the real lesson I was taught.

As I stood in line, I again learned the power of cruel words and the way they shape a man's view of his fellow neighbor. I stood there in line waiting to check out, and as I did, I overheard a conversation. The middle-aged woman in line seemed to know the cashier well as she addressed her from line, asking, "Did you see the State game?"

The cashier replied, "Yeah, I sure did. It was a shame we lost."

The middle-aged woman responded, "Well, if we did not have such a crappy quarterback, I do not think we would have."

The conversation ended here and it may have been because the cashier knew who I was, or it may be because the Lord was willing to spare me from further torment. In either case, I was very thankful it did end, but I was not unaffected by its sharp thrust. The thrust of those words cut right into my heart and continued to stir the fire which had begun earlier. The continual bombardment of harsh words against me caused my heart to be so very hard toward everyone in the community.

Although it is a natural reaction to put up a wall when flaming arrows are being shot through one's midst, I found if I did not really care about the people who were hurting me, then I would not be hurt myself. They were trying to tear apart my hopes and dreams. All the achievements my life was centered around were being attacked and I was not about to let my life go. I felt if I gave into their attacks, I would be conceding my very identity. I was built on the fact I was a good football player and a great athlete. If they wanted to attack, I would make myself so strong they could not penetrate me.

The attacks brought on a shift in who I was. I was no longer receptive to public opinion or optimistic about their thoughts. Instead, I thought I knew their thoughts, and I was of one mind: to prove them wrong. I began to think the world was attacking my identity and I was the only one who could fend them off. So that is exactly what I began to do– fend them off.

CHAPTER SIX

The Defense of a Girlfriend

§

Now Saul's daughter, Michal, was in love with David, and when they told Saul about it, he was pleased. "I will give her to him," he thought, "so that she may be a snare to him and so that the hand of the Philistines may be against him." So Saul said to David, "Now you have a second opportunity to become my son-in-law." -1 Samuel 18:20-21

When attacked, all people take up a defense so as best to preserve their health and wellbeing. In ancient times, people would build very large walls around their cities in hopes of protecting themselves from attacking enemies. The United States has set up an intricate missile defense system in order to block any attempted attacks from foreign soil. After a crushing loss in the State Finals and so many attacks on my dreams, I set up defenses as well. I built a wall to keep the enemy out and I set up missile defenses to protect my interests.

The walls of ancient cities consisted of blocks so large that many still remain from thousands of years ago. My wall was five feet, seven inches tall, with dark brown hair, and a beautiful smile. I met her my freshman year of high school. Joy was in my science class and every day was a trial in order to see if I could resist her intoxication. Joy was one of those people who naturally drew in others. She was by far one of the prettiest girls in class and, knowing my goal was one of "All-American Boy" status, I wanted nothing less than the prettiest, most alluring girl in class. I pursued her all my freshman year with every intention of making her my girlfriend, but in actuality what I sought was for her to be my wall. I did not fully understand what it would mean for her to be my wall, as I had not yet experienced all I would over the coming two years, but I had enough experience already to know I needed protection from the world.

The "All-American Boy" is always a favorite of the ladies, but only if he truly embodies the character of an "All-American Boy." I discovered the girls one might attract attention from as the "All-American Boy" were not always the girls with the best moral reputations. Luckily, Joy was not one of those girls. At the time, I thought having her as a steady girlfriend would help protect me from these kinds of attacks as well.

Case in point, I was only a freshman when I started to play baseball on the varsity team. Those were hot games in the spring in South Texas; both the pressure and the sun made the sweat roll down our faces. We were playing an out-of-town game as I walked out of the dugout and began to warm up in the on-deck circle. I took a nice smooth cut and turned toward the stands. As I looked up, I saw two beautiful young women staring at me from the fence. They had walked over as I began to warm up. They were both very pretty and smiled quite warmly at me. I could tell they were both seniors and I was just a freshman.

Now, any time two beautiful senior girls approach a freshman boy and start to smile, there are a certain number of nerves that develop. The conversation that followed was what caused me to be aware of the wall which I needed to establish. "Hi, Andrew," the girls said in unison as they smiled at me from the fence.

Without any eloquence and a little stutter, I managed a, "Hello."

The girls both smiled, realizing the effect they had on me, and one of the girls smiled a little bigger as she said, "You sure do look good today."

Not knowing what to do, I simply smirked and swung my bat again. Still smiling, the other girl looked at me with a smile and one eyebrow raised as she said, "I think you need to come home with the two of us tonight. We have all sorts of things we would like to do with you."

Turning all kinds of red, I turned back to the game realizing that I had an at-bat to go to. I was not exactly sure if they were serious or just joking, but I soon learned they were more than likely serious. See, baseball game bus rides have a way of bringing out stories that would never be heard otherwise.

If we think our children are being kept innocent, we are surely mistaken. There are things that go on in this world I am still amazed at and disgusted by. I only say I am disgusted because just as easily as those who take part in these activities, I, too, am just as easily seduced. I would listen to the sexual exploits of all my teammates during those years on the bus. I did not have any of my own at the time to discuss, but I was very much involved in listening to theirs.

I heard of teenage kids involved in orgies and public sexual acts at parties. I heard of girls giving themselves to guys they were not even dating, much less married to. There were pictures of these events that were brought on the bus to enhance the storytelling. It became a show and tell of pornography many times. I am not really sure this is a new occurrence. From what I have heard, locker rooms have been like this for some time, but these bus rides and these two girls made me aware of the dangers that lurk right outside my town, or in this case, within my own soul. I knew I wanted to be popular with the girls, but I did not want to be as popular as many of my teammates were.

There was another danger I perceived that caused me to want a wall of defense, and that was the partying that went on all the time. All the alcohol consumption and exploits of many of the people around me were looked down upon by my parents. One of the motives for being the successful man I wanted to be was the approval of my parents. I had always looked up to my parents as great people, and even though I did not always want to be under their supervision, I still wanted their approval. I needed to separate myself as much as possible from the stress of having to deal with all of the different kinds of attacks that would occur, so I decided to find someone of like goals to invest myself in and shield my personal life from the things I was so desperate to avoid.

In order to achieve this goal, I needed to convince Joy she wanted to date me. This was a harder task than I was expecting to encounter and I am sorry to say I did not use the best judgment in accomplishing what I wanted. When I first met Joy in science class, I also came to find out she was dating a young man on the football team with me. They were dating, but it was a very interesting relationship, as it was forbidden by her parents and they were not actually allowed to go anywhere together. I did not see this as a real relationship and as much as I now regret it, I pursued her despite her affiliation with this other young man. I must say I am very sorry for my actions now that I look back with clearer vision. The pursuit of our own desire despite the needs and desires of others is never a good thing. It is a hard lesson to learn to put others before oneself, and at this point in my life I was not able to do so.

I pursued Joy for over a year before I was finally able to convince her to be my girlfriend sophomore year. She agreed to go out with me with providential timing, because it was the night before the State game she decided to go to the movies with me. The problem was she was still supposedly dating the young man on my football team. However, we went out for a short evening, and a few weeks after the game she broke up with her boyfriend and began officially dating me. I was overcome with excitement at her finally choosing me.

It was in Joy I found my protection from the world. She became my best friend in high school. We spent almost all of our spare time together and we loved to be together. Because I had my best friend with me and we could entertain each other, I never had to engage the public I now resented and feared. I could hide within my walls and not worry about those who lived outside of them. We emotionally invested our souls in each other. It is a dangerous thing to invest one's soul in someone before one is married, even if it is not in the ultimate physical act of making love. I found protection from the outside world with Joy, but I was not protected from the threats inside the walls of my own soul. We were connected in an emotionally intimate way and without the bonds of marriage, we were setting ourselves up for a tremendous fall.

I wish I could go into great detail to explain the pain which I have caused to myself and to Joy, but I simply cannot here. I find it interesting what we do to those whom we love. It is so often humanity takes that which it loves and uses it to its own advantage in ways that should never be done. I should have been a minister to Joy and her family, but instead I was simply a poor reflection of what I could have been to them. Joy and I attended different denominational churches. She was Catholic and I was Baptist and I knew this was a problem. It was mostly a problem because I was running away from my faith, hiding in her, and not listening to the guidance of God.

I loved her and I was kind to her, except for the fact I neglected the greatest kindness I could give her. I did not share with her the relationship God had given me. I did not allow her to be a part of the beautiful communication I shared with my Lord because I was neglecting my relationship with Him during that time of my life. My heart breaks at the thought of my actions. Oh, that the Lord would forgive me for my actions of selfishness.

Love those whom God gives us, both the ones who are easy to love, like Joy, and those whom are extremely hard to love. God is love and He should be reflected in all the relationships that bless us. It is hard to tell how we should love those around us. Love thinks nothing of personal gain, but is always giving. Yet we so often think love is something we take. We take from those we love and neglect to appreciate what we receive. Let us not build walls around ourselves with the people we love.

We cannot hide from people, for we are called to minister to them.

It turns out I never needed a wall, because my Lord's love was the only wall I needed. It is hard to see the strength of our God when all we look at is the army on the ground. God's people must be people who gaze toward the heavens, for when our gaze is set on the ground we destroy ourselves and those we love. Destruction comes from inside and outside our walls for those who do not look for protection from above. In this life, protection comes from who we know, but I was slow to learn of His power.

CHAPTER SEVEN

The Defense of Strength

§

Then Saul dressed David in his own tunic. He put a coat of armor on him and a bronze helmet on his head. David fastened on his sword over the tunic and tried walking around, because he was not used to them. "I cannot go in these," he said to Saul, "because I am not used to them." -1 Samuel 17:38-39

I have a tendency to try to protect things which I am completely incapable of protecting. This would not be such a bad quality if it did not cause me to be exasperated at the fact that I am unable to manipulate that which is out of my control. Proverbs 16:9 says, "In his heart a man plans his course, but the Lord determines his steps."

It is hard not to confuse planning with the placement of one's steps. In an attempt to protect the placement of my own steps, I fell into the trap that captures so many Americans. It is only a natural progression that those who are strongest would be weakest in their pride. Self-assurance is only good if the information one bases that assurance on can be found reliable. I am assured of one thing: I control my heart and nothing else.

I was in love with Joy, but I was also still in love with football, and even more in love with vindication. I wanted more than anything to prove I was the man I knew I was. I believed I was strong and I would prove to the world all I was capable of achieving.

My junior year of high school was characterized by injury and disappointment. The coach who took us to the State Finals left for a bigger school and, due to certain pressures, my new coach forced Mighty and me to rotate in at quarterback. We rotated every play, which is never a formula for success. The rotation caused me to feel even more pressure to rise to the top. Unfortunately, when my time came and Mighty flunked out of football, I tore all the ligaments out of my throwing thumb. I was still able to play, but the thirst of my vanity was only grown by the predicament of my junior year.

When an athlete is hurt in what some would consider a small part of the body, the consideration for how it might affect his play is severely diminished. The public has a short memory when it comes to the events of those people in the spotlight. My thumb was in a splint all year after Mighty flunked out. It was torn so badly I could not grip the ball without it popping out of place. No one seemed to realize or remember what had happened to my thumb. I was labeled as a quarterback who could not throw and to inflict more pain on my already scarred pride, my team, which was ranked number two in the state, lost in the second round of the playoffs.

I think it is a common vice of people to want everyone to think well of them. Why are we dependent on what other people think? We are only affected by what others think if we believe their opinion to have some bearing on reality. One does not get upset when strangers are thought ill of, it is only when a reputation of close relation is attacked that resentment proceeds. In my own life, I have come to realize I react this way because I believe I am not complete. There is something in the depths of who I am telling me I am not all I should be. There is a voice haunting my soul saying I am scarred. My inadequacies dictate I should be upset when someone points out a flaw in me, whether true or untrue. In any accusation of imperfection, the realization I am not all I should be is brought to the forefront of my mind. After two years of accusations, I began to realize what my second level of defense should be. I developed a resolve to have my strength lie in the extent of my perfection.

I began to train going into the summer before my senior year. It was the hardest I had ever trained, although I must confess the extent of my previous work ethic was poor at best. My sweat had but one purpose, and that purpose was to quench my vanity. I worked so I might be strong, and in my strength protect myself from the attacks of those who would say I was less than perfect. It haunts me to acknowledge the little amount of faith I had then and still have today. I believed my strength would protect me from the pain my soul felt at the realization I was not perfect. Only a fool believes in a rope he knows to be broken, but I am sad to say I was that fool.

Most fools are blind to their folly until after the damage has been done. I basked in my foolishness to the extent my abilities let me. My work paid off that summer in many ways. My first opportunity was presented to me at a Nike® combine in Austin, Texas. Nike® combines are a great opportunity for players to prove their abilities before a wide audience of people. The best players in the nation are extended invitations to be evaluated.

There are a series of tests that are administered at every combine in order to evaluate the players who have potential for colligate athletics. The combine consists of a forty-yard dash, 5-10-5 shuttle, vertical leap, and bench press evaluation. After strength and speed are evaluated, there is a chance for the players to show off their football skills. The players are placed on the field and given drills to run.

I grabbed my shirt as I stood in the heat waiting for my chance to prove myself in evaluation. My shirt said Nike® on the front and the way in which it clung to my body gave me a sense of excitement that is only felt by one who waits in anxious expectation. It is hard to describe the feelings that arise as an athlete is surrounded by so many talented peers. Each athlete is pitted against the other for the prize of being the most touted on the field. There is competition on the outside, but the competition within is the biggest struggle. There is a certain tension that occurs as one waits to engage their body. There is a feeling of potential that sits within the soul of every athlete, and whether or not that potential will be reached is the greatest stressor an athlete can feel.

The heat was stifling, but it seemed to only warm my muscles and my hopes I might perform. I had hopes of setting myself apart and above all of those around me. As I got down into a stance to run my forty-yard dash, all I thought of was how I needed to perform. The look of puzzlement that came across the timer's face as I separated myself from the group was exactly what I was hoping for. I looked over to my dad after I ran and held up four fingers. I had run a 4.4 second forty and my hopes of defense in strength were coming to fruition. As I crossed the line in the 5-10-5 shuttle, the coach looked at me and asked, "Who are you, Son?" I answered, and as I did I knew I had done my job.

I had made an impression, and with that impression came the approval I desired. It reinforced the idea I held then that life is mostly about what people think of others, because if the right people think the right things, then a person is deemed successful. One can become strong simply because another person says he is strong. I knew this was true, because when others say a person is weak, then that person ends up, say, in the line at movie shops with people trashing his name.

My plan for defense in strength continued to be successful after Nike® camp. The success I had at Nike® camp led to an invitation to the University of Texas summer camp. Summer camps were another form of evaluation and separation, and any chance to separate myself from the prospect of being labeled weak was an opportunity I would take.

The week of the Texas camp started off pretty exciting and would end up the same way. I drove to Austin on my own that week. Austin was not far from my house, only about an hour and a half. It was a short trip, but it was not a trip I had taken often on my own. Austin is a beautiful city, and downtown is one of its most beautiful attributes. The downtown area of Austin is home to both the State Capitol and the University.

As I maneuvered around downtown, I finally found the private dorms in which we were to stay. I turned the corner and as I did I started to hear honking and waving from all the drivers around me. I had expected a warm reception at the camp, but this was more than I could have hoped. There was a good reason, namely because this was not a welcome. I had started off my camp experience by driving down the street in the wrong direction. I realized I was going down a one-way street the wrong way just in time to jerk my car into an adjacent parking lot. There is something annoying about one way streets, they never seem to go the one way a person wants to go.

I made it off the one-way street and onto the football field. It was on the football field I continued to improve my defense by strength. Once again it was the turning of a timer's head that reinforced my plan. The timer at UT clocked me and once again asked my name. It was rumored I ran the fastest time at camp, but the coaches were reluctant to give it to me because they did not think I was capable of it.

I proved myself again in the shuttle, running a 3.9 second 5-10-5. With my shuttle time and my forty time, I had gained the attention of the coaching staff. The coaches at UT wanted me to play cornerback, but I had never really played defense. Despite my reluctance, I went ahead and worked out for them.

I had the kind of success I was hoping for. Mack Brown came and spent time talking to me. Having the head coach of Texas tell me I was a Division I athlete was exactly the kind of accreditation for which I was hoping. I ended up bruising my knee during the time I spent working out on the field. With a bruised knee and a lot to prove, the fastest man competition was at hand. All the coaches wanted to see if I was as fast as they thought I was, but what they would see was how fast I was with a swollen knee.

My knee felt pretty bad, but there is something about the atmosphere that surrounds someone under pressure that helps him overcome pain. Perhaps it is the atmosphere of a large stadium with the lights on, the feeling of hundreds of kids lining the field waiting to see who will come out on top, the knowledge that on the field where a person runs, games have been played that defined the legacy of great players. It came down to me and one other guy, who was a tall, athletic wide receiver and pretty fast. We got down in our stance, and with the cheers of all our peers to push us, we ran. With a bum knee I ran and with a bum knee I finished second. It was second, but it was still status and most of the coaches were impressed with my performance over the week. I had reassurance I could depend on strength.

CHAPTER EIGHT

A Second Encounter

§

In the course of time, David inquired of the Lord. "Shall I go up to one of the towns of Judah?" he asked. The Lord said, "Go up." David asked, "Where shall I go?" "To Hebron," the Lord answered. -2 Samuel 2:1

If life is a stage and we are all but merely players, one might think we would be more aware of the script. It seems more likely we are fish in an aquarium, completely unaware of our purpose. It is when we are most engaged in swimming in circles the Lord sees fit to pull us out of our water. I was thoroughly consumed with establishing myself as a dominant athlete the summer before my senior year. However, God was thoroughly involved in moving me toward other ambitions.

There are a few things in life I really love, but rest assured, long bus rides are definitely not one of them. It seemed every year my church youth group went to summer camp, it involved a long bus ride. It was a twenty-hour bus ride to Nashville from Cuero, but we were all excited to be headed to camp. Every year we went to camp was a good year. Camp was the highlight of my youth group experience, because it seemed for at least one time every year, camp would bring a real experience with God. The summer I spent at Mission Fuge in Nashville, Tennessee was no different.

I went to camp with the mindset of getting away, but also with the mindset I was still a dominant football player. I found my identity and strength in football and that assurance stayed with me wherever I went. My soul rested in success and my success rested in pigskin. I got to camp and the first thing I did was to find a pick-up game with anyone I could rustle up. It is a sign of insecurity for a person of high talent to try and display their gift by using those with limited means. Insecurity may be the cause of many faults in young men, because it causes them to act like fools in front of girls, as well as lord things over those among them whose talent lies in a different area.

Unaware of my insecurity, I went on with camp in a normal fashion. I went to a housing project in Nashville and played sports with kids, I attended worship services every day, and had the normal summer camp high from worshiping as a large group. I even met the usual unbelievable camp girl. It was a normal camp experience.

I once saw a girl's profile on Facebook that said, "Normal is just a setting on your washing machine." I have learned in a life watched over by our Lord, normal is most definitely reserved for the washing machine. It is only through eyes obstructed by the methodic that life appears normal. To those who lift their lids to see, a world of such variety appears that normalcy no longer reserves a place in Webster. Our God does not deal in normal, but moves with the extraordinary. The only thing routine about life is the dark surface of the back of an unconscious person's eyelids. When one truly sees the world, life's grandiose parade of characters turns normal into spectacular. It must be seen that the immensity of changing detail dictates that nothing is normal, nothing is routine. There is boredom in normalcy, but there is excitement and joy in the extravagance that is our God and is our life.

I sat with my eyes glazed in a sanctuary filled with youth; we sang and I sang with passion. Singing has a way of taking hold of someone even when he or she is not fully walking with the Lord. When one is a child of God, it just seems right to sing to God. It is as if something deep inside calls a person to praise God even though that person might not be following through with the life God has called him or her to lead. I sang and then I listened as a young man brought the Word of God to us. I do not remember his message, but it suffices to say the presence of God was upon him, because God began to speak to me. I sat and listened, and God began to whisper, *Bow your head.*

It was just a feeling in my body, but I remembered from younger, better times and I bowed my head. I began to ask God what it was that He wanted from me. He had not asked for anything, but it was on my heart there was something I should give. As I prayed, I began to encounter God again as I did when I was younger. It started with feelings and impulses, and then something began to swell inside my heart.

At the time, I did not know what it was, but I could feel it. It was a feeling of comfort and familiarity, as if I had been in this place before. I felt warm and yet scared, but I was not scared as if frightened for my life, but instead shrunk down to a proper place. It was as if I was a child in a play pen and my parent had just entered. I felt protected and yet in awe of the immensity in front of me. As I prayed I felt impressions of communication, *Will you concede? Will you go?* These phrases appeared on my heart and I knew exactly where they were coming from.

Lord, where will You send me? I asked as I sat in silence. Thoughts began to roll through my head at such a rapid place I could not keep up. A picture of a map appeared in the forefront of my mind and I began to move from region to region. I was entertaining the idea of being sent to all of these places. When one speaks with God in this fashion, there is always a fear God is not speaking and one is manipulating. This fear began to come to mind as I sat there in that sanctuary. I thought, *Lord, please guard me from choosing myself. Where would You have me go?*

As I called out to God, all the places that seemed hardest to go began to come to mind. I always feared Africa as a child, and Africa came quickly to my mind. Not far behind Africa was China, but it also passed. Then my mind was brought to a place I had never considered before: Israel. I had not thought much of Israel in previous times, but my mind was centered upon it. I cried out internally, *Lord, is this of me, or is it of You?* I waited for an answer and my mind did not sway away from Israel.

Looking back, I would think I should have been very upset by this revelation, but it did not seem to disturb me. There was a disturbance in my soul and it had arisen from a call I felt from the time I was 5. My call to serve the Lord with my life had begun to arise within me once again, and I was very much afraid. I did not know what to do. Should I stand? Should I sit? Should I pray some more by myself or should I seek counsel? I had never been in this situation before and I had no idea what to do.

I decided the burden on my heart was too much and I had to share it. I got up out of my seat and headed for the back of the sanctuary, and went straight to my pastor. I knew he was in the back and, although we were not particularly close, he was who I felt I should talk to. I found him and quietly asked him to go outside, and as we went outside, we found a bench to sit and talk.

My pastor's name was Dr. Robertson, but we sometimes called him Brother Glenn. I began to inquire of him, "Brother Glenn, how do you know if God is calling you to the ministry?" Brother Glenn looked at me and began to describe his own personal call. He took me through his college years and a rebellious time in his life. He described how God laid a call on his life and he gave up the pursuits of fraternity life and took up His call.

My pastor really opened his heart to me in a way I had never heard him do before. He went so far as to describe an experience he once had with Christ himself. I had never encountered God the way he described, but there was something about the way in which he opened up to me that was comforting. There was something in the way he described his experience that resonated with me. His experience was not my experience, but there was something in his manner of speech, something which led me to feel he knew the place of which I spoke. Brother Glenn had been to the place of comfort and fear and he allowed me to feel that he had been there.

I graciously thanked Dr. Robertson for sharing his experience with me, but I did not leave having surrendered to the ministry. Instead, I went on with camp and did not deny I had an experience, but I was not willing to let on how powerful it had been. I was changed from that "normal" night at camp, but I did not share how much. I left with the mindset of contemplation. I was on good terms with God. I would think about His proposal, but there were girls and sports and I was not ready to sign up yet. I would soon discover that when one is drafted by God, holding out of camp to renegotiate one's contract does not work so well.

CHAPTER NINE

The Season of Testing Comes to Us All

§

Hear my cry, oh, God; listen to my prayer. From the ends of the earth I call to you, I call as my heart grows faint; lead me to the rock that is higher than I. –Psalm 61:1-2

It is in the pinnacle of pride the presence of God can move over a person with such strength that it seems as though one might drown. The man who has been moved to great heights is also the man who is capable of great plunges. After my summer success, I was on my way to greater heights than I had ever experienced. My climb had taken its toll on me, but I was determined to get the best out of all the adversity that seemed to come my way. As the football season began, the opportunity to climb to a position that was defensible from all attacks was at my fingertips and I was not about to let it slide through them. The prestige that was brought on by the good evaluations of the summer would only carry me so far and I was well aware of the fact I must still perform.

My senior season started with all the expectations that came with a class that had done so well in prior years. We started the season ranked in the Top 10 in the state in class 3A. I moved through the beginning of the season with ease, and fully expected to dominate the field any time I walked out of the locker room. For the most part, that is exactly what took place the first two games of the year. I had worked very hard to be in control of what happened to me on the field, and this domination I was able to achieve while I played was my protection from all that might attack me in the world. My identity, my dreams, and my hopes of fulfilling the "All-American Boy" role were all wrapped up in my ability to control what happened on the field.

There is a progression that takes place in our life, whether we wish it to our not. At some point in our experience of existence we find we have elevated ourselves to an inappropriate position. This revelation comes to all people at different times. For some, it seems to come with such ease it might almost be inherent to their very nature, while others are blind until a rather strong shaking of their foundation causes them to examine the ground upon which they stand. The unfortunate few are those who do not see until their sight is opened with a light that comes only from death. For those unhappy souls, the sight of the truth brings the wrath of God and the fire of hell.

I felt as though death would soon ensue as I stood on the sidelines. My heart pounded and ached with the pain that was swelling up from the scars on my heart. The heat from the field was melting into my body to combine with my anxiety, which turned into a series of shakes and trembles. I found myself in Sealy, Texas with all my desire to control my prosperity in shambles. Sealy was a powerhouse in 3A football. They had won more State Championships in past years than I cared to count. Almost every State Championship had come at the expense of my team, as we had lost to them in the quarterfinals and semifinals, but we had never beaten them. My senior year was the year we were going to beat them for the first time. We were ranked higher than Sealy and they were in the middle of a down year. The Sealy game started as the perfect opportunity to improve my stock as a premier player. The game started with great expectations, but it would soon turn downhill. We could not score and Sealy put two touchdowns on the board before we scored at all.

In the fourth quarter, I had my chance to put us on the board. We had moved the ball down inside the 20-yard line, and I could taste the end zone as I got under center. The thoughts of the play started to run through my mind as I approached the line of scrimmage. We had called an option play to the right side of the field and I need to evaluate my chances of being successful. I looked down the line and everything looked good. We had position on the corner of the field and as I took the snap, I sprinted at the corner.

I moved quickly, and as I did, the corner started to open up. I had a clear field all the way to the end zone. My hands were in the normal option position as I sprinted down field, both hands were on the ball and the ball was in the middle of my chest with my elbows bowing out. At any moment, I was ready to pitch. Now, I knew pitching was not needed, but my hands remained in the option position, just in case. As I ran, the defense pursued me, but I knew there was no hope of them catching me before I broke the goal line. I was just a few yards out, about to score, and the hopes of winning the game were about to be revived. My legs were pounding in the ground and my mind was racing.

What happened next is mostly just a blur. I was ready to cross the goal line and claim my touchdown when all of a sudden, the ball was gone. The ball had been firmly in my hands and now it was shooting out the back of the end zone. I was helpless as I watched the ball bounce in front of me. I was running, but the ball was moving faster than it was possible for me to move. With each bounce, the hope we would win seemed to move farther and farther from my grasp. I could not stop what happened. Somehow, in the middle of my sprinting, the ball bounced off my leg and went through the back of the end zone. Instead of a touchdown and hope of winning, I was left with a turnover and devastation. Sealy got the ball on the 20-yard line and we did not get any points.

I moved to a remote portion of the sideline while the defense took the field. The death of my dreams was so heavy on my soul I felt as though I was going to be crushed. I began to be tormented by thoughts of the State loss. I remembered the all negative things that had happened to me. I remembered the way people looked at me and the things some people said to me. I remembered the disappointment I felt in my own heart. It was too much for me to bear. I could not bear another experience of curse words written on my car. I would not be able to handle the town being disappointed with me again.

It may seem melodramatic for me to be at the point of tears over a football game, but one must consider what football was to me. Football was my life and my dreams. Football was my town and my history. The game was so intimately intertwined with who I was that the loss would be like a knife searing into my heart. I kneeled on the sideline and bowed my head in prayers and tears. Prayers and tears are where many people find themselves when presented with a wound that seems as though it might kill them. Prayers and tears are always available, but are so rarely utilized in a world that has its mind set on the fight in front of them.

As I prayed, I was taken to the place in which the Lord reserves for those special encounters. It is the most intimate of intimates, and it is what drives the Christian soul. In my prayers, I searched for the One who might help. Crying quietly, my heart burst forth, *Lord, help me! I cannot take the pain that is going to come.* I looked to the sky just above the stands on the opposite side of the field. My heart raced, but I waited until it all faded away. The noised quieted and the lights dimmed as I was taken away. In my solitude, I began to speak again, *Lord, will You not help me from this circumstance? I know You can, but why do You wait?*

As I sat, the voice of God moved through my heart, *Andrew, why should I help you?* I felt a brief moment of shock, but it was not given enough time to culminate. God continued, *Why should I listen to you when you will not listen to Me? You do not do what I ask, why should I grant your request?*

Many thoughts of telling God I would consider His request started to come to my mind. For years, God had been asking for all of my life and I had refused to comply. I always had a good reason or an excuse to wait. I began to regret my decision not to listen harder to the Lord. I had no answer to give other than, *I am sorry.*

I sat and continued to wait and as I did the feeling of, *Do as I ask,* began to creep into my heart.

I began to realize the situation arising out of this turmoil. I spoke up, *Lord, I will do as You ask. Wherever You want me to go and whatever I should do, You have all of me. Please help me now and I will do as You ask.* This time I did not tell God I would think about it. I told Him I would do it. In the heat of the moment, I meant it with all of my heart.

God did not give me a verbal answer, but a feeling began to spread inside of me. I knew we were going to win. I do not know how I knew, but I knew. I did not think about how we were going to win, I just got up and felt at peace. It was a peace words cannot do justice to; I was in a trance with nothing on my mind but what I needed to do in that moment.

After my fumble disaster, the defense made a stand. We got the ball back, but with five minutes left in the fourth quarter, we were down by 14 points. In some sports, five minutes can be a long time, but in football five minutes is usually just enough time to score once. The atmosphere in the stadium was only intense inside the bubble that surrounded me. The fans had moved into the relaxed state that comes with thinking the ending of a game is secured. Some of the Cuero fans had even begun to leave the stadium. One of my dad's colleagues left just before we took the field. Despite the lack of crowd enthusiasm, I felt overcome with focus and determination. There was so much on my heart and mind that looking back it seems more like a smothering fog than any discernable feeling or thought.

I walked to the huddle with a familiar play on my mind. There were certain plays Coach liked to call in tough situations, and the tight-end screen was one of them. My tight-end's name was Derrick, and he was not only a friend, but also a talented player. Derrick was about six feet, three inches tall and weighed two hundred twenty pounds. Derrick also moved really well for such a big guy, and Coach wisely liked to use him in our offense. The only trouble was the other team knew our tendencies in this particular situation.

As I approached the line I did not notice the defense approached the line strangely. The defense did not give away they knew the play, but as soon as I snapped the ball it was clear they were looking for exactly what we were running. I dropped back to pass and the line let the defense through just as they were supposed to do. I continued to drop back, but some of the defense did not follow me. Instead of following me into the backfield, two defensive players followed Derrick down the line of scrimmage. There was nowhere to throw the ball, because they were waiting for the pass to Derrick, and my linemen were downfield, which meant the pass could not cross the line of scrimmage. There were two defensive linemen following me, and I had to make a move.

I stuck my foot in the ground and gave them a shake and I was off. My linemen were already downfield to block for Derrick in the screen, but now it was a quarterback draw and I was in the open field. I made one move and there was only one man between me and the end zone. We had started with the ball on the 20-yard line, and now only the safety remained between me and an eighty-yard touchdown run.

I would like to say I broke the safety's ankles and took off, but I think it is more accurate to say that he got scared and fell on his own. In either case, I broke loose and eighty yards later we were one touchdown closer.

Eighty yards should not seem like that long to a seasoned athlete, but it felt like an eternity on my lungs! By the time I reached the end zone, I was hardly jogging, but I had outrun everyone by so much it did not matter and I scored. My lungs hurt, but the excitement of the crowd was revived and the hope of our team was sparked.

The offense went back to the sidelines and we waited to see if the defense would give us a chance to tie the game. It seemed like only two minutes of rest on the bench before the cry of the special teams coach was heard, "Punt return!" I was still out of breath, but not enough to make going out on the field an irksome thought. I jumped up from the bench and proceeded to run out with my team. We had returned the punt to our own 35-yard line and we now had two minutes and sixty-five yards to go to tie the game. It was an amazing defensive stand, but our stagnant offense needed something beyond amazing to score in two minutes.

Other than the few brief runs, our offense had been dormant all night and now we were asked to take the ball down the field when the defense knew we had to move quickly. The first three plays of the drive where unsuccessful and we were left with a fourth down and long. The coach called a timeout with the game on the line and very little time left in the game. We approached the sideline where I should have been very nervous about what was going to happen, but I was too tired to be scared or concerned. Coach looked at us and turned to me and his son, Will, who played wide receiver, and was also someone with whom I had thrown quite a few balls. Coach asked, "Can ya'll run the play you ran in 7-on-7 this summer?"

7-on-7 is a passing game for football teams to play during the summers, and we had a very successful year in 7-on-7 the prior summer. We had gone to State and done quite well with the exception of a couple of plays. One of those plays was the one I knew Coach was referring to as soon as he asked. We had developed a trick play, a "hook and ladder", which we decided to run in the State tournament and it was intercepted for a touchdown. Will was the receiver who always got the play, and when he looked at Will I knew what he wanted to run. We both looked at each other and nodded our heads that we could do it.

The "hook and ladder" was a dangerous play because I had to take a quick three-step drop, and then throw to Will on a hook route. As soon as Will caught the ball, he had to pitch it backward to another receiver who would be running behind him. We knew it was dangerous, but we did not object to running it, even though we had never practiced it in pads, or in a real practice. We took the field after the timeout and the game was on the line.

It is strange how important moments pass. I dropped back to pass on fourth down and threw a strike to Will. Will caught the ball and another wide receiver, Val, ran behind him. Will was hit in the back right after catching the ball, but he was able to get the pitch off just in time. Val caught Will's pitch and turned up field. Val was fast and he took off running at an angle toward the sidelines, trying to outrun the defense. Val was pushed out of bounds, but not before he crossed the first-down marker.

We had new life, but not much time. I dropped back to pass and looked for Derrick again. This time I was able to find him and the line did a great job of giving me time. Derrick was running straight down field and I connected with him on a long pass. We were now within striking distance, but we were going to have a hard time getting into the end zone. We had little time to score and the defense now had a condensed field to help guard the end zone. We began to run pass plays and the defense was bringing a rush. On the first play, I ended up having to scramble, but I came back to the huddle after a modest gain completely out of breathe. Looking up at my linemen, I declared my need for help, "Guys, there is no way I can run anymore, you have to keep them out of the backfield."

We lined back up to pass and the defense came again. I slipped out of the pocket and took off toward the sideline. I knew I needed to get out of bounds and stop the clock. I ran even though my body was screaming for me to stop. I dove for the sideline just as I was being tackled. I had stopped the clock, but we were still short of the end zone and there was less than one minute left in the game. I came back to the huddle and I did not have to tell the guys I could not do that again, because the look that was covering my body said enough.

I dropped back to pass on third down and threw a fade to the right side of the end zone. The ball fell right through the hands of Brandon, a young receiver with great promise. We did not think long about the fade to the back of the end zone before we ran the same play again. This time, I threw the pass to the left side of the end zone and Val was there waiting for the pass. Val had turned the shoulders of the defensive back, because he was scared Val would get behind him. I lobbed the ball just short of the back of the end zone and right at the back of the corner. Val jumped over the back of the cornerback and, in "White Knight" fashion, grabbed the ball out of midair and landed both feet in the end zone. We were now within a point of tying the game.

The extra points in all our games were always something of a concern. Our kicker was able to kick the ball very hard, but he kicked with his toe and the extra point was never a sure thing. This extra point was going to determine the game and as he put his foot into the ball, I heard the crowd roar. I was on the bench, but I knew the roar meant we were tied and now going into overtime. I sat on the bench and tried to refresh myself. Stephanie, our trainer, attended me while I sat on the bench. I was shaking and really tired, but also pretty happy we were now tied. Stephanie brought me water and the look in her eyes told me that she was concerned about me. I was shaking like a leaf. The overtime period brought more for me to shake about.

The format of overtime had just been changed to the colligate format. Each team would get a possession from the 25-yard line and a chance to score. The first team to outscore the other team in a succession of two possessions would be the winner of the game.

We lost the toss and Sealy got the first possession. Our defense had been amazing in the second half, but a little low on steam, they allowed Sealy to score. Sealy quickly put the extra point through and we were down by 7. We had to score a touchdown with our possession, or the game was over. We drove the ball down and stalled out about ten yards short of the end zone. After three very unsuccessful plays, we were back to fourth down and goal to go. The game was on the line again, and the ball was in my hands.

The play was called and it was an option pass with a corner route out of the backfield. Garrett was our fullback and he was going to run the corner. I took the snap and faked the option, then I dropped back to pass and as I did, Garrett headed to the corner of the end zone. Garrett was right on the goal line when I zipped a pass to him. Garrett jumped into the air and caught the pass right as the defender hit him in the legs. Garrett was fond of doing flips into the end zone and I was never as happy to see him do it as I was when he flipped backward into the end zone right then. We only had to make the extra point to go into a second overtime

The extra point team ran out onto the field and I ran to the bench. There was a high probability we might miss the point, but in the depths of my soul, I knew we would not lose the game. Without the fear of loss, I did not care to watch the extra point, because I was sure we would make it and there would be a chance to win the game. As I sat on the bench, the kick went up and God proved again that He does things the interesting way. The kick was blocked! It would seem the game was over except for what happened as the ball was in the air.

Sealy was overcome with excitement because of the block, and as they celebrated, one of their players tried to catch the ball. What he forgot in all the excitement was a blocked kick is returnable, and as soon as he tried to catch it, the ball would be live. His attempted catch turned into a divine disaster. The ball went right through his hands and right into the hands of a promising wide receiver. Brandon fell on the ball in the back of the end zone and scored a 2-point conversion. I have never seen officials leave a field so fast.

As soon as Brandon recovered the ball the game was over. We had won! Brandon ran across the field with the ball up in the air. Our team and our fans went crazy. We had players doing cartwheels and coaches screaming like little kids. I found myself on a knee in thankful prayer. What the blocked kick and Brandon's miraculous recovery conveyed to me was I was overcome with the "Cinderella effect". I felt a sense of the miraculous all around me. The change in the tide of the game could not be anything but miraculous. It was more than just how the game changed, it was the way in which it changed within me.

The entire time I was playing, my body was acting crazy, but my soul was dazzled by a promise: God had given me slippers. God had given me a mystical means of changing circumstances that seemed far above my head and I had the opportunity to watch. When one is taken from despair to delight in the whirlwind of providence, there is nothing to do but smile and say, *Thank you.* Salvation deserves thanks and on my knee on a field in Sealy, I learned that valuable lesson.

CHAPTER TEN

Painful Promises

§

I will be his father, and he will be my son. When he does wrong, I will punish him with the rod of men, with floggings inflicted by men. But my love will never be taken away from him, as I took it away from Saul, whom I removed from before you. -2 Samuel 7:14-15

Covenants with God are very serious things. The modern child does not understand the meaning of a promise. We have grown up in a society where, if something is not written on paper, it is not legally binding, but more of a suggestion than anything else. On the field in Sealy, I do not think I consciously thought my promise was a suggestion, I just thought all the stipulations of what I had agreed to were negotiable. God was calling me to give all of my life and I was willing to consider giving parts of it to Him. Deep within me, I wanted to give more than just parts, but there were other things pulling on sections of my heart.

The biggest pull was football. I do not think it was really football that was pulling me from my call. I think there was an ideal I strived for that was ingrained in the deepest part of my mind. I wanted to be the "All-American Boy". I wanted to be successful. I have spoken ad-nauseam about what it means to be the "All-American Boy", but it really boils down to the need to fill a hole.

We all have holes whether we are American or Iraqi, German or Chinese. There is a part of us that needs to be filled. We long for success because we long for love, and love is what we think success brings. We long for security because we long for the feeling that comes when entangled in the arms of the one we love. Sometimes we find love in success or security, and sometimes we do not find love at all. The saddest sojourner is the one seeking that which they already have. I am reminded of the experiences I have had looking for sunglasses, which I mentioned at the beginning of my story.

Everyone has experienced the desperate hunt for sunglasses that unknowingly sit upon his or her head. The hunt for sunglasses always ends in humiliation and exasperation when someone else has to tell the person with the glasses he or she already has what he or she is looking for. I believe the hunt for success and all those other extensions of love that are found in the silly pursuit of "hole-filling" are nothing more than a journey to retrieve what is already in a Christian's possession. The non-

Christian tries to fill the holes of his or her heart with water that evaporates as he or she pours, but the Christian continues to block the water as an endless pitcher pours it out. I tried to block the love of the Lord after the Sealy game, but I soon found one cannot block the flow of a waterfall.

My plans to be successful were proceeding as planned on the football field. The team had experience a bump in Yoakum, but other than one loss, we were well on our way. I was racking up individual stats at a rate I knew would draw attention. I was recording well over one hundred yards per game, both rushing and passing. After our first district loss, we were rolling through teams like a steam roller, and I had great plans, including scholarships and State Championships.

I had not forgotten my discussion with God on the field in Sealy. I knew He had taken care of me and I was going to make a concession. I had decided I would take a mission trip to Jordan the summer after my senior year, which seemed like a good idea because it seemed like a way to appease my calling without having to give up the future I had longed for so desperately. I was going to listen to the voice of God, but only with part of my heart. The other parts were reserved for me.

It was the seventh game of the year when we arrived in Edna, Texas. Edna was not a great team that year and we knew it. We got off the bus and continued on to our normal pre-game ritual. We all headed to the field to walk up and down and dream of the glory that would come that night. Edna was a little town with a small stadium about an hour from Cuero. As we walked onto the field, I noticed something different about the turf: it was not well cut and a little uneven.

Usually, we kept our grass really low to make running as easy as possible. Most teams kept their grass cut low, but this field was not well-kept. Although I was not happy about the long grass and uneven turf, it did not really surprise me. We were a fast team and anything another team could do to slow us down was to their benefit. I briefly noted the long grass and continued on with my dreaming about the things to come that night.

As game time grew closer, I fully expected to have great numbers and a great win. Edna was one of those teams I knew could not stop me or my team, and we took the field with that knowledge in mind. Edna won the toss and elected to receive the ball first. Edna was not great that year, but they did have one weapon.

Edna's running back was a guy I always raced in the 100-meter dash in track. He was a fast guy, faster than I was in the 100. Pretty big, too. The first drive was a "hello" from Edna's running back to our defense. Edna scored on their first drive, but I was not worried, because the defense was now off the field, and it was my turn to take over.

We took the field and ran a couple of running plays. We did not go for substantial gain, but we were still in good position. Then, when a play came in that put the ball in my hands, Coach called a bootleg. I was excited as

I took the snap. I rolled out to the left side of the field and looked down field. I had my tight-end open down the field, but everyone had run off to keep me from throwing. I decided to take off.

I turned up field and everyone left their receivers and came after me. I stuck my foot in the ground and gave a shake to the first guy. He fell down, but the left side of the field was being converged upon and I decided it was time to reverse field. I quickly cut back to the right side of the field, and as I did, a line of my teammates came to seal off the pursuing defense. There was a series of strong blocks and I was free to take the corner. I got around corner and headed up the right sideline. It was now a foot race and there was no way they were going to catch me. I strode up the sideline, high-stepping into the end zone.

We tied it up and the very next offensive possession for Edna ended in a stall. We had the ball and now I had the chance to take the lead. We began to march down the field, headed for another touchdown. We were well inside Edna's territory when the play came in from the sidelines, and it was an option to the left side of the field. It was a chance for me to take us into the end zone and I was about to capitalize.

I took the snap and sprinted to the left. Everything was in my hands and I was about to take control of this game. As I sprinted left, my line sealed off the corner and I had an open field. I sprinted up field and was met by a defender. We were one-on-one in the open field. It was a situation in which I loved to be. There was no way this guy would stop me. I came straight at him and got ready to shake him. I quickly stuck my toe in the ground and gave my body the normal roll to one side. As I turned to come back the other direction, something happened. I felt a snap and then a sharp crack.

I was on the ground and the ball was no longer in my hands. I did not care that the ball was gone. I did not even think about the ball. The other team's sideline was right beside me and they were screaming and cheering in excitement. I laid on the ground grabbing my knee. My knee was not hurting, but it was the closest thing to grab, and I took hold of it. It was shock at first, and then I began to scream. It was only a natural response. My leg was on fire and my lungs were letting the world know it.

I laid on the field for what seemed like a pretty long time before the trainer showed up. They lifted me off the ground and supported me under my arms. I had to get off the field and they began to help me walk on one leg. Stephanie, our trainer, asked me if I could put pressure on my foot. I tried and as soon as I did I collapsed in pain. I could not put any pressure on it, much less walk.

I hopped over to the sideline where I proceeded to plop down on the bench. I sat on the bench while my dad took off my shoe and sock. He had come down out of the stands as soon as he realized I was hurt. He began to examine my leg as I sat. All of the people in our stands were watching me as I sat on the bench. I was not really aware of their stares. I was starting to feel funny.

At first I felt hot and then I started to feel dizzy. Dad continued to mash on my ankle and as he did, I lost it. I began to throw up profusely all over the sideline. My mother would later tell me everyone kept asking her if I was having stomach problems before the game. I did not have a stomach bug, but my stomach was responding to the pain and stress in my life. My stomach still has a strange way of dictating to the world what is going on inside me. As I threw up and my dad examined my leg, my coach came over and asked how I was. Coach addressed my dad, "It is just a sprain right?"

Dad responded with the dejection that can only come from the certainty of something bad, "No, it is definitely broken."

In so few words and a divine touch on the ankle, all the plans I had so elaborately developed where changed. My leg was broken and my thoughts started to swirl. The voices in my head were those of the coaches at the University of Texas, *We really need to see what you are capable of on the field this year.* I knew my plans for big-time football were dependent on me playing. Now, I was headed to the hospital and my team was left without me on the field.

My dad decided to drive me on his own to the hospital and he quickly loaded me in the back of our car. Other than the throwing up, I had tried to contain my emotions. I did not want the world to see what was really building inside of me. Even in the car, I did not want my dad to know how I felt.

It is a hard thing to be vulnerable, even when we are in the presence of the ones we love. I laid in the back seat as we left the stadium. My chest started to burn with the emotion building inside of me. I thought of all the expectations of the people in the stands. I thought of all the people who thought I could not be great. I would venture to say I had an issue with thinking the worst of people, except I would later find out my fears about what people were thinking were somewhat grounded in reality.

Right after I left the stadium, my girlfriend's mom sat in the stands near a group of men. One of the men began to speak rather loudly, "Finally, that white boy is gone. I know we have other kids who can run just as well as he can." It was nice to know later my girlfriend's mom wanted to deck the guy, but restrained herself.

I knew people were thinking things like that man in the stands. Those people had been in the stands my entire high school career. They never wanted me to forget who I was: a rich white kid, not one of them. They never wanted me to forget we lost State when I was a sophomore. My heart hurt because their thoughts echoed in my head as we drove.

Yet, there was a sense of relief in all the hurt. Somehow, I was relieved all the pressure was over. My relief did not outweigh my grief, however, and even though I tried so hard to contain it, I began to weep. I cried and hurt and my dad listened. "Dad, I just want to play college football!"

Dad tried to comfort me, "You will get to play, Son, you will."

"I know, but I wanted to play big-time football," I responded.

Dad tried to encourage me, "Maybe you will get well fast enough to play again."

Dad's efforts were good and I felt a little better, but I knew once again I was to fight an uphill battle. I began to forge in my mind the idea of fighting the odds again. The voices of the people in the stands fed my need to prove myself and I was going to do it.

That night in Edna, Texas a spark was lit that had nothing to do with my need to prove myself. There was a spark lit that was part of a divine plan to consume me with the passion of God. The hearts of men have a tendency to get dry. When things are dry, they burn, and that can cause people to seek water. God had water He needed to give me that He wanted me to share with the world. In Edna, Texas the course of my life began to be set ablaze. The degree of heat which I would experience was yet to be seen. I did not see the intervention in my life. I did not feel it, nor did I care to. I continued to pursue my plan while God pursued my promise.

CHAPTER ELEVEN

Running Without Seeing

§

Jonathan said to David, "Go in peace, for we have sworn friendship with each other in the name of the Lord, saying, 'The Lord is witness between you and me, and between your descendants and my descendants forever.'" Then David left, and Jonathan went back to town.
-1 Samuel 20:42

My sister has this miniature wiener dog puppy named Hector. Hector is a pretty good dog, but he has some bad habits. One of the things Hector does, I completely do not understand. Hector loves the trash. He will try and get in the trash any time we are not looking. The thing I do not understand about Hector is that he will climb up on the trash can and then he will get yelled at or whipped, but then he will go back and do it again. Hector will climb in the trash no matter how many times he gets in trouble. Hector wants that trash so bad he does not care how many times it hurts him. The bag of garbage my sister and I throw away is the very stuff Hector will risk a beating for on a continual basis. Often I ask myself, "Man, how stupid can that dog be?" Looking back at my life, I think it would be a good question to ask, "Who says that same thing about me?"

* * *

After the Edna game, things progressed slowly. The football team continued to win, even though the defense did most of the scoring. My leg did not fare as well as the team. It did not want to heal, and after a couple of weeks in a cast, I ended up on the operating table. I had to have screws put through my leg, which meant I would be out for the rest of the season. I knew it was a bad thing for me and for the team, and I hoped the team would have success without me, but their victory was only moderate compared to the hopes at the beginning of the season. I watched from the sidelines as they lost in the first round of the playoffs. It was a sad, frustrating affair to watch my team lose in the first round of the playoffs my senior year, but there was nothing I could do.

My frustration in football gave me the motivation to want to transform back into my old self as fast as possible. The broken leg and lack of exposure on the field left me in the very predicament in which I thought I would end up. I was shunned by all of the major schools, but there was still hope. The Naval Academy and a few other schools wanted me to come play for them. I had a chance to go to a school that was not all that great and prove I was a star. I was going to show all those schools that gave up on me I was not all washed up. I knew there was still hope; I just had to work hard.

Back when I was in junior high school, I attended a summer camp called Camp Longhorn. I remember right before I went to camp there was quite a to-do over whether or not I could swim. I assured the people running the camp I could swim and went on my way. I did swim fairly well. I could swim with any of the other kids in our local pool and did not think twice about my competency as a swimmer. I knew I was not proficient in all the strokes, but I was not attending a swimming camp and I knew I could swim well enough to have fun.

However, that year at camp, I learned there was a great difference between swimming in a pool and swimming in a windy lake. We were expected to swim a great deal in the lake at Camp Longhorn, and by the time camp was over, I hated swimming. I found out swimming against the wind and waves was a lot harder than anything I had done in a pool. It seemed like every time we jumped into the lake, I would swim and everything around me was pushing against me. I gave all I had in that lake and I seemed to go nowhere. Many years later after breaking my leg in Edna, Texas, I soon found out pushing against God's will is a lot like trying to swim in a lake. It is only good for getting tired and frustrated!

Hard work is the American ideal, and a good one at that. Hard work is what I felt would put me back on the track I intended to run. My senior year of high school was moving downhill quickly, but I thought I could do anything if I put my mind to it. After breaking my leg, there still remained a whole world of people who did not view me as successful. It is what we are taught in this world, that we need to be successful and that hard work is how we get there.

After considering the merit of hard work, I think we instill it in our children because it is true to some extent. Hard work does bring some types of success in this world. Man has made great strides by hard work. The Egyptian's built the pyramids with hard work and the Chinese built the only manmade structure that can be seen from space with hard work. There is no doubt in my mind hard work has merit, but I think a question must be asked of our hard work: To what end do we work?

I was ready to work after I broke my leg, and to a very specific end. As I think back on my intentions, I am reminded of a section of a book by my favorite author. In the seventh book of *The Chronicles of Narnia*, C.S. Lewis writes concerning a group of dwarves, "The dwarves are for the dwarves." The end I strove so hard for had an echo in the background. My heart was driven by the intention, "Andrew is for Andrew." I wanted desperately to show people something. I wanted to show myself something. I could make myself great, and the world would marvel at what my hard work constructed. There were expectations that had been piled on my shoulders. Not by anyone specific, but by the world in general. I was to be the "All-American Boy" or I was to be a failure.

All I thought I should be had helped to make me resentful of all I thought the world saw me as. Resentment is a powerful tool of the enemy against the saints. Resentment can clog the hearts of a believer to the point God must slap a person in the face in order for him or her to hear Him. It is the blessed who are slapped. When the silence of resentment continues on over the course of time, the heart hardens and the mind forgets. I think forgetfulness may be one of the most dangerous propositions for those who love the Lord. We must remember the great deeds of Christ Jesus and we must unclog our ears, lest we find ourselves wandering in a world with no meaning.

Unaware of my own deafness, I began to train. At first, I was restricted to weightlifting, because my ankle was still preventing me from playing sports or running. I was crippled, but I was not about to let that small fact stop me from indulging in the pursuit of myself. I hit the weight room, but it was more like a slap with a wet noodle than a hit. One day after school, I went into the weight room and began to lift with my two best friends, Ryan and Blake. We hit the bench press first, because when one is in high school that is the cool lift.

Blake and Ryan were both considerably stronger than I was, but I did not let that upset me. I had been sidelined by injury, and I was never the strongest guy in the weight room. What did bother me was what happened as I got under the bar. I began to press up some weight and as I did I was exasperated. We got to a weight I had done six times the summer before, and I could not even do it twice.

I could not believe it. The guys were spotting me and they sensed I was upset. Ryan quickly tried to intercede, "Andrew, do not worry about the weight. You are just out of shape and have not been working out." Blake quickly, but calmly, threw in his approval of Ryan's hypothesis and we went on with the workout.

The incident on the bench press was upsetting, but not as upsetting as when we started to work on our backs. It was really hot in our weight room as we lifted. The weight room was a new addition to the school and it was pretty nice. It had an indoor workout area and a considerable number of weights. The new building had one serious flaw, and that was that it did not have any air conditioning. There were a number of sliding doors, which could be lifted up, and two large air fans, which were supposed to create a kind of wind tunnel in the room. The only problem with wind tunnels in South Texas is the air is already so hot the wind is more of a reminder of the heat we had to endure.

That afternoon was no different than most, and it was really hot as we lifted. We had removed our shirts as we started to work out on the lat-pull machine. As I got on the machine for my turn, the guys watched me from behind. After just a few reps with very little weight, Ryan and Blake both said something that really bothered me. I am not sure which one said it or if they said it together, but the words followed in this fashion, "Andrew, man, you are skinny. You better not let the girls see you with your shirt off."

It gouged me in the side. I knew they were right. I had lost a lot of weight. I was about ten pounds lighter than I had been. I only weighed 167 pounds to start with, and the ten-pound loss was dramatic. I did not understand why I seemed to be shrinking, but I shrugged it off and thought it must be because I was not lifting.

The weightlifting had not been going well, but I soon forgot about it because I got cleared to use my ankle. It was the middle of basketball season, and I had a good chance to help my rehab out on the court. I was not a great basketball player, but I was fast enough to help the team out. I got an air cast and hit the court. The season did not go so well for me, or my team. I seemed to be at least a step slow all the time. I had a broken ankle, what did I expect? It did not seem that out of the ordinary, but I got pretty frustrated with not being up to par. My frustration began to move to a higher level with the last basketball game of the season.

I had been under the weather with bronchitis just before the game, but it seemed to have subsided and I was ready to try to help our team win. The game was just as frustrating as my lack of ability had been. We were getting beaten by a team we had killed earlier in the year. It was embarrassing, and my playing was embarrassing. I was running as hard as I could and yet I seemed to go nowhere. I could not catch my breath and guys were blowing by me. It was only the second quarter and I felt like I was running a marathon.

I finally looked to the sidelines and yelled at my coach, "Coach, I have to come out." I never liked coming out of the game, much less when we were losing, but I did not have a choice– I did not seem to have any gas. After that game I was really upset. I was not lifting well, I was getting sick, and then I was not able to play basketball. My idea of working myself back into a position of success was not going as I had planned.

Basketball season came to a close, and baseball and track gave me new hopes of establishing myself. There were great expectations for me in both track and baseball. I had started on varsity baseball since I was a freshman and I had played well all of those years. Baseball season started and I played pretty well. My batting average was over .400 and I was playing well in the field. I did not quite have the strength to hit the long ball like I had in years before, but it had been a hard year on my body.

Track proved to me the year had been harder on me than I thought. Track was a sport in which I had excelled for my entire high school career. I had gone to State both my freshman and sophomore years. Some bad luck had caused us to miss State my junior year, but my senior year was going to be amazing. I was a sprinter and a long jumper. Individually, I was a great long jumper, but as a sprinter I was more of a relay man than anything else. I ran a good hundred meters, but never well enough to finish any higher than fourth in a very fast district.

I enjoyed winning in track and the prestige that came with winning, but I could not stand track practice. I went to practice despite my disdain because I knew it would serve me well in my pursuit of winning. We would always run as a team. The relay team would get in a line and take off with the strongest runners leading the way. I was always in the back of the pack at track practice. I was in the back not because I was slow, but because when I say I was a sprinter, I mean my endurance was awful. I could beat just about anyone in the first forty yards of a race, but after about forty yards I started to give out.

Endurance was never my strong point and I did not mind running in the back at practice as long as I was running in the front of a race. Track practice killed me my senior year. I started in the back and I finished even further in the back than usual. It did not surprise me because I was out of shape, but it sure did make practice awful. I loathed every second of practice, but soon the first meet came and I had a chance to make it all worth it.

The first meet of the year was at a small school called West Oso. West Oso was just outside of Corpus Christi, Texas and a fair drive from Cuero. We arrived on the bus as usual, which was always an adventure. The first event I had was the long jump, which I was excited about. I loved long jump and knew I should be better than almost everyone I faced. The competition opened, and I was ready. I found my marks and waited for my run at the pit. I bounced up and down on my toes as I readied myself for my approach. I bounced once, then twice, and I was off.

I hurled myself down the track as fast as my legs would carry me. I hit the board and exploded. It felt good. I had great height on my jump and as I sailed through the air I held my legs up as long as possible thinking, *I am back. The old me is back and I am going to smoke these guys.* I landed in the sand and collapsed to my heels just as I was taught. I had an excellent long jump coach named Coach Pope. He had been a great long jumper in college and was a great guy all around. Coach Pope had taught me well, and as I stepped out of the pit I knew my form was good. I was expecting a 23-foot jump or better.

The officials called a mark and began to measure. After a few seconds of waiting they called out 20'11". The frustration was back. That distance was a good two feet shorter than anything I had expected. I did not really understand, but I did not let it bother me too much. The next two jumps were the same and despite my own disapproval, I won the long jump. I figured it must be the wind that made my jump short. The meet was held just off the coast and it is always windy down there. I quickly forgot about how short my jump was and was happy with the fact I beat everyone else at the meet, so my mind moved to the running events.

The first event I ran was the sprint relay. It is hard to tell how fast someone is running on a relay because all the splits can run together when the baton is being handed off. Our time was not great, but once again, I thought it was probably the wind. Next came the 100-meter preliminaries. The 100-meter was another event I was thought to do very well in. I was always a little too slow to make it out of the district, but this was my senior year, and despite the fact whoever qualified from our district went on to State, I thought there was a good chance I could make it. The speed I had shown on the football field had held many to believe I was a favorite in the 100-meter. I had never run any faster than a 10.8 in the 100, but this year my coach thought I would break 10.6, and so did many others.

I approached the blocks in my heat for the preliminaries. When a person is one of the fastest guys on the track, prelims are never a big deal. Most of the time, preliminaries are just an opportunity to get warm for the finals. I knew no one in my heat was likely to beat me and so did the guy next to me. As I got in my blocks, the guy on my right looked up and said, "Man, Heard, why do you have to be in our heat? You will make us all look bad."

I wanted to be polite, so I replied, "Well, I am still kind of hurt, so I doubt I will win that easily." I mostly said this out of courtesy because what was really going through my head was, *Man, am I going to smoke these guys.*

We got in our blocks and the starter called out the count, "Runners to your mark, set, go!" We burst out of our blocks. The start was always my best part of the race. As I shot out of the blocks I knew everyone would be well behind me, but as I looked up I found something I was not expecting. I was not leading. Not only was I not leading, but I was in the back of the heat. I felt adrenaline start to pump. *I cannot lose my heat.* I tried to kick it into gear, but I could not seem to move. I strained and pulled, but I could not catch up. Everyone was pulling away from me and there was nothing I could do. I crossed the finish line in disbelief.

What had happened? *Maybe it was just a really fast heat?* I quickly made my way to my coach and asked him what the time was. His answer hit me in the stomach so hard I almost threw up. He said, "I got you at an 11.9." I could not believe it! 11.9 was a time I ran in junior high and not even a good one at that. Girls ran faster than an 11.9. I began to think maybe the time was wrong, but it was not.

My pride was crushed! As I said before, a young man never wants people to see him cry, and as I felt tears start to well up inside me, I knew I had to leave the field. As calmly as I could, I made my way back to the stands. There was a group of blankets and pillows our team had left under the stands for relaxing in between events. I headed straight for the pillows. I did not dare to look to the right or left to see who was around me. I found a pillow and stuck my face in it as fast as possible.

I laid there for quite some time. I did not understand what was going on. I had worked hard and I should have been doing well. It seemed like everything that could go wrong was going wrong. My heart could not take it anymore and I just let out all the tears that were burning in my heart so vehemently. I did not know what to do, so I just laid there. I had other races to run, but I could not move from that spot. I just stayed there hoping everything was a bad dream and I would wake up.

Finally, Coach Pope showed up and tapped me on the shoulder. I will never forget how he knew what to do in that situation. I was devastated and he knew it. He did not try to ask if I felt okay, he simply tapped me on the shoulder and said, "I scratched you from the rest of your races." I was so thankful! No one could have said anything nicer than he did right then.

I did not know why I was so slow, but I sure did not want to run anymore that day. My head hung lower that day than it had in a long time. I found my dad and asked him if he would take me home early. The ride home was hard, but Dad found ways to help me think it was not as bad as I thought it was. Dads are good for that sort of thing.

It was not long after that meet that I had track practice again. I really did not want to go this time, but I thought if I was that out of shape, I had to go. We ran fifty second runs on Mondays. Because of the fifty second run, Monday was the worst day of the week for me. A fifty second run meant we would sprint as hard as we could for fifty seconds, then when time was up, we were expected to have come as close to finishing one lap around the track as possible.

My lack of endurance caused me to hate this kind of workout, but I had to do it, so I got in line as usual. We took off and I was at the back of the team again. As we came around the first curve, I was really tired. I thought, *Andrew, you are so out of shape, keep running.* I continued to run past the 200 marker, but everyone was leaving me way behind.

I did not care how slow I was running, I was just trying to finish. I thought if I just kept running, I would get in better shape. I made it to the 250-meter mark and I ran into a wall. My whole body shut down. I could not run anymore and I just stopped. Not only could not I run, but my chest was killing me. I bent over and rested my hands on my knees. I started to heave and I could not stop. My chest was burning and now I was hacking. I could not stop hacking and then I started to taste blood in my mouth.

It was not long before Coach was by my side asking me if I was okay. I said, "Coach, I have to go see my dad at the hospital because something is wrong with me." I thought maybe I had pneumonia or something since I had been sick a lot that winter. Coach Pope looked concerned and thought it was a good idea if I went to the doctor, too. I left practice that day thinking, *There has got to be something wrong with me.*

I began to think back over the past couple of months. Basketball had been weird and so had weightlifting. I began to think of how much my chest had hurt recently. My dad thought I had pulled a muscle in my pec and so I took some Vioxx, an anti-inflammatory drug, every time my chest started to hurt. The Vioxx seemed to work, so I figured the pain was indeed a pulled chest muscle, but now I was starting to wonder.

I thought back to the West Oso track meet the week prior and how poorly it had gone. I remembered a specific incident before the 100-meter. I had not run as well as I thought I should have in the sprint relay and so I decided to stretch really well before the 100. I asked one of my coaches, Terrance Friar, to stretch me extra well so I would be loose. Coach Friar agreed and we proceeded to stretch.

I remembered when I was stretching, Coach had rolled me on my back and was stretching me by lifting up my legs. All of a sudden, I could not breathe. I coughed a few times and rolled over. I did not think much of it then, but as I left track practice that Monday with blood in my mouth, I wondered even more if there was something wrong with me.

I left the high school and made my way home. I was a little concerned about my health, but hoped it was nothing bad. I told my dad what was wrong and he said I should come and get an X-ray the next day because I might have had pneumonia. I figured he was probably right and I showed up at his office the following day.

We took the X-ray and my dad and another physician looked at it. Dad said I did not have pneumonia. I was pretty confused as I left the doctor's office that day, but there was nothing I could do about it. I did not understand why my body was acting the way it was if I did not have pneumonia. I concluded I must be really out of shape and needed to work harder.

After the trip to the doctor's office, I went to school the next day and then to play a baseball game that night. It was a beautiful evening and I was glad to be in Edna. Edna was the town I broke my leg in while playing football, but it was one of my favorite towns for baseball. Two years before, when I was a sophomore, our baseball team went to Edna and I hit three homeruns in one game. I almost hit four, but one was caught at the wall. During that same game, my coach did something I will never forget. Coach came up to me after I hit the first two homeruns and, right before I stepped up to the plate for a third time, said, "Hit it out of the park."

Telling a player to swing for the fence was something I had never heard a coach do before, but I smiled and turned to the plate. I remember thinking, *I am going to take this right over the left field wall.* The pitcher threw the pitch, and *BOOM*, I slammed that ball right out of the park.

As I came around third, I will never forget how Coach said, "You're the man, Heard, you're the man!"

That glorious game was strongly on my mind as I planned for a repeat performance on this night. I was currently hitting well in baseball, but I had yet to hit a homerun. I thought for sure I would hit one in Edna. The night went well and I ended up 3-for-4 at the plate with two stolen bases. I thought my performance had not been too bad for a guy who had gotten sick at track practice the day before. However, I left feeling concerned about one event that took place that night.

I had come up to the plate knowing I could rock the guy pitching. It was my last at-bat and I had wanted to hit a homerun. I knew I should not have been think about trying to hit a homerun, but in that park I knew it was alright. As I stepped into the batter's box, I had the same eye on the pitcher I had two years before as a sophomore. He threw the first pitch and I smacked it.

As soon as I hit it, I knew I had hit it as well as I could. I turned to watch the ball fly over the back wall, but just as it was supposed to leave the ballpark, it died. The ball fell right into the hands of the left fielder and I was out. I could not believe it. I had hit the ball as well as I could, and it was not a homerun. It did not make sense, but the night was successful overall, and my Dad cheered me on from the sideline. I will never forget how he cheered and smiled at me as I played. That kind of unwavering support is something I will never know if I am capable of providing!

CHAPTER TWELVE

Moved in a Different Direction

§

And Jonathan had David reaffirm his oath out of love for him, because he loved him as he loved himself. -1 Samuel 20:17

The bus ride home after the Edna baseball game was a memorable one. As I mentioned earlier, high school baseball bus rides are often a very interesting adventure filled with young men bragging about how great they are, their stories of sexual conquests, and many exaggerations. This particular bus ride had a different conversation than all the ones preceding it. For some reason, I rode the bus that night and felt moved to converse with my friends about what God had been laying on my heart.

I was very much concerned with the fact high school was about to be over and we had never shared time in Christian fellowship together. I felt the call God was placing on my life had a good opportunity to be answered on the bus that night, and I started to ask the guys what they thought about meeting in the mornings to pray together. To my surprise, the idea of praying together was met with great warmth. After a good conversation about what we should do, we decided to meet the next morning at the park to pray before school. I was very excited at the opportunity to do some good in the lives of my friends.

I arrived home from the game that night and entered the living room of my parent's house with great excitement for my plans with my friends the next morning. My parents both sat in the living room looking rather serious. I thought it was a little weird they were just sitting there staring at each other, but I just assumed they were waiting to talk to me about the game. We talked about the game and how well it went for a little while. After our conversation started to dwindle, Dad looked at me very seriously and said, "Andrew, I need you to come by the hospital in the morning before you go to school."

I looked at him funny and said, "Sorry, Dad, tomorrow is the first day of a prayer meeting with the guys. I cannot come tomorrow, we will do it later." I thought surely it would be alright if I came some other time, but appointments are the most important thing when one's dad is a doctor at a hospital.

Dad firmly looked back at me and said, "No, Son, you have to come tomorrow." I did not understand what the big deal was. I was aggravated, but after a few minutes of arguing, I decided I would leave the prayer meeting early and head to the hospital for whatever it was I had to do. Dad assured me that it would not take long, and so I conceded.

It is hard to sleep at night when so many things are running through one's mind. I did not really understand what was going on with my dad. He told me there might not be anything wrong, but a radiologist had examined my X-ray and it looked strange. Dad thought most likely the X-ray was just poorly taken, but we had to be sure. I laid in bed that night and wanted to think there was nothing really wrong with me, but there was a strong feeling in the back of my mind I was sick somehow. I hoped Dad would figure it out tomorrow and I would be on my way back to being my old self.

The stress that came with uncertainty and the excitement of doing something truly good the following morning caused my pillow to seem like the most uncomfortable rock upon which I was ever caused to lay. I had felt for so long I should be involved with my friends spiritually and tomorrow was finally bringing the opportunity to do just that. I was frustrated I would have to leave the prayer meeting early for the hospital, but at the same time, I thought it was good I was getting checked up. I finally fell asleep that night with a range of emotions running through my head and a hope that tomorrow would go well.

I awoke the next day and got dressed quickly. I had so much to do that morning and I hated to rush through getting ready, but I did not have any choice. I made it to the lake to pray, but it seemed like I was only there a few minutes before it was time to leave. Unhappy about having to leave and pretty scared about going to the hospital, I left my friends and made the short five minute trip across town.

The hospital was a place in which I had spent a lot of time, and yet is was a place that never quite agreed with me. It did not really represent anything good in my mind. The hospital was the place that always made my dad leave. I had spent more hours than I cared to waiting on Dad to deliver a baby, or see an injured person in the Emergency Room. I knew the hospital helped people, but it seem more like it just sucked everything fun and good out of my life.

I arrived at the hospital and found out I was going to have a CAT scan. Even though I had never had a CAT scan I was not overly concerned with the procedure. I once had to have an MRI and managed to survive that, so I figured the CAT scan could not be much worse. After changing clothes, I was led to the scanning room and had a rather unpleasant experience with the I.V. they had to start for the scan. I never much cared for needles, and right before they stuck me, I was not sure if I was more scared of something being wrong with me or of being stuck with the needle.

Despite my doubts, I survived the stick and found myself lying on my back while a funny doughnut of clicks and swirling noises rushed around my body. As I lay on the examination board, I began to think again of all the strange things my body had been experiencing. It began to hit me how much my chest had been hurting. The pain in my chest never occurred for extremely long periods of time and I never had really thought about the pain much until I found myself on my back, getting examined by this weird machine.

I waited for the test to be over and thought about the basketball trip I had taken a few months earlier. We had played an out-of-town game that night, and we were driving back. Everyone was trying to sleep and I was doing the same. A memory came back of a sharp pain shooting through my chest. The pain that night was pretty sharp and it lasted for a few minutes. At the time I thought, *Wow, that is one heck of a pulled muscle.* It was now occurring to me maybe it was not a pulled muscle. I lay there waiting for the examination to be over and hoping harder than ever there was not something seriously wrong with me.

The test finally finished and I was ready to find out what was going on with me. Most people would not have thought they could find out the results of a test right after the test was done, but I was a doctor's kid and I thought I would know right away. I quickly made my way to the technician's room where my dad was waiting. We looked at the pictures and I asked, "Well, how do they look?"

Dad looked at me and responded, "I am not the one who reads these things so I cannot tell you, but ask the technician."

I quickly turned to the technician who was now glancing up at me. "Does it look normal?" I asked.

The technician looked at it for a while and said, "Yeah, it looks pretty normal to me."

A sense of relief came over me I had never experienced before. Dad told me to go change and head back to school. I made my way back to the doctor's lounge where I had changed, and as I walked down the hall, I was all smiles. I felt as if somehow I had won a great victory and yet I really did not do anything.

I emerged from the dressing room with the same sense of victory with which I had entered and proceeded to walk the length of the hospital to my car. As I walked the halls of the hospital, my feeling of victory was soon eclipsed by perplexity. I began to ask myself why, if I was not sick, was I performing so poorly in my sports? Why was my body hurting the way it was?

I did not understand what was going on in my life. I was very happy to not be sick, but at the same time I was devastated by it. Being sick was a chance to explain why I was performing so poorly. If I was not sick, then there was only one other explanation: I was just not any good anymore. The thought that my athletic ability had left me was more than I could take. I walked out of the hospital no longer feeling good, but in a dreadful state of depression. *I might not be the man I should be...* I left for school with the hope that maybe if I worked harder, I might come back from this hole in which I found myself, but I was still left with a strange feeling I could not shake.

The rest of the morning went along in a normal fashion. It was still my senior year, and while class was not particularly exciting, I was enjoying the time anyway. Lunch time rolled around and I had an unusual surprise—my sister, Rene, went to lunch with me. My sister was a freshman and she almost never went to lunch with me. Our school had off-campus lunch and Rene did not have a car, but she always found a friend to ride with instead of me. I once asked her why she never rode with me and she stated simply, "You're too boring to go to lunch with." It made me laugh more than anything, but on this particular day, Rene had decided to risk the boredom and go to lunch with me.

Lunch was quite unremarkable, but when we got back to school we were welcomed with a visitor. Our principal, Mr. Kelly, was waiting for us at the front of the parking lot. Mr. Kelly was a young man and I was particularly fond of him. For a principal, he was a really nice guy. He was clean-cut and had a very nice wife who had been a teacher of mine in elementary school. Mr. Kelly was one of those men most people just generally liked, and I felt the same way. As we approached the school, Mr. Kelly did not look quite as happy as he usually did.

Rene and I approached, and as we did, Mr. Kelly called out to us, "Rene and Andrew, could you come with me to the office?" As soon as he called us I knew what had happened. Rene and I were not the kind of kids to get in trouble, and even if one of us did, the likelihood of us both being called to the principal for disciplinary reasons was slim to none. There was only one reason we could be called to the office together, and I knew exactly what it was.

I am not sure if Rene knew the reason we were walking to the office, as I did, but she was quiet and did not ask any questions. As we walked, a sense of calm came over me. Looking back, I think the appropriate response should have been terror. If I knew all that was to come, I am sure terror would not have been the only word I used, but I did not know and my soul was quiet. It is quite remarkable how God works. God always lets us know exactly what we need to know to see whatever it is He wants us to see. God never burdens us with more than we can take and He never leaves us without enough to focus our thoughts.

As I walked the halls of my high school, God interceded in my life and the lives of those I loved by bringing me strength and clarity. I knew what was waiting ahead of me, and I did not waver. I cannot say what happened next was of my own strength, for a rational mind unaltered by the divine would never behave in such a way. It must be said the actions I took were not my own, but the work of the Holy Spirit. God himself embodies the Christian, and when a saint is too weak to stand, it is God who holds him up for the world to see.

Rene and I followed Mr. Kelly to his office and he motioned for us to go in. As I opened the door, I was hit by a wave of emotion that can only come from a child seeing his parents crying. My eyes began to tear and I reached out quickly to embrace my parents. I did not need them to tell me why they were crying because I already knew the answer. Long before that morning, somewhere in the deepest part of who I was, I knew something was wrong with me. I did not know exactly what it was, but I knew it was there. My parents' tears now only confirmed what I had long thought to be true. I had not wanted to believe it for a very long time. Now, cradled in my parent's arms, I knew I could hide from it no longer.

After a few minutes of crying, my dad looked up at me and began to let it out. "They found something on the CAT scan after you left," he said. Dad was still red in the face, but he kept talking, "There is a tumor in your chest and it is pretty big." My mom was still crying and Dad continued on, "The mass was hiding behind your breastbone and that is why we could not see it. They think it is as big as a fist." A knot started to swell in my throat, but I fought it off. My sister was crying at a gushing rate and I had to put a stop to the hemorrhaging.

Looking at my family I said, "It is okay." They kept crying and I continued, "It is okay, God will take care of me." It sounds like something anyone would say in a time of great crisis, but I was not saying it just to say it. I was emotional because my parents were hurting, but deep within my heart I knew what I had just proclaimed was true. I was not worried about the tumor. God had answered my prayers before, and I knew He would not leave me alone.

I let my parents finish crying and then they asked me what I wanted to do. I did not know what I wanted to do. What does a person do after he has just found his parents crying in his high school principal's office? What does he do after he has just found out he has a tumor in his chest? Dad said I would have to go for more tests the next day in Victoria. Victoria is a town just east of our little town, and it had big enough hospitals to have all the doctors and machines needed to examine me properly. After finding out there was nothing to be done until the next day, I decided to stay at school. I figured at least at school, I did not have to think about my situation the entire time. We hugged one last time and my parents left and my sister and I went back to class.

Classes were hard to concentrate on after such an emotional experience with my parents. Really difficult situations are hard to share with people whom one is not intimate, and yet when something of such a caliber is upon one's shoulders it shows all over his face. People can tell when a person carries a heavy load even if he tries his best to hide it. One might wonder why I would hide something as significant as a tumor at such a young age, but it is the most elementary social custom to hide things that are uncomfortable, no matter how much it burns in one's chest.

It is odd how society works. One tries so hard to make the life of his neighbor comfortable. It is socially acceptable to conceal the weakness that lies within each of us, and yet we only lie with our mouth. One says, "Yes, everything is fine," with words, but we are so much more than words. Communication scientists say that 90 percent of our communication is nonverbal and it is hard to cover all 90 percent of that communication. It is not just hard, it is impossible when the weight on our heart is great.

The human heart speaks in tones which the ear cannot hear, and yet we lie without the mouth. The turmoil and weakness we wanted so hard for our neighbors to avoid is thrust upon them with the most powerful form of communication we have within ourselves. Our hearts betray our social responsibilities and we put the people around us in a more awkward position than if we would have revealed the truth from the start.

When we carry great burdens and lies about the hurt, it causes those people who might help us to feel as if they are unwanted. People are placed in a position of wanting to respect the fact we lied in order to prevent their knowledge of our hurt, when they clearly know exactly how much we hurt. I was a bundle of contradiction when I went to class that afternoon, and people saw right through me.

In my first class after lunch, I entered the room and for all intents and purposes did nothing and said nothing the entire time. It was as if I was there, but I was somewhere else. The class I had after lunch was Photography, and it was always an entertaining class due to the friendly banter which occupied our time. I was too heavy and too deep in thought to engage in my usual conversation. There were two people in that class who noticed my state and were willing to step outside social boundaries to find out what was on my heart.

Social boundaries are a tight rope to cross. A little to one side or the other, and there is no telling how far one might fall. It is the fear of falling that keeps us gulfs apart from the other people with whom we walk through life. There was a young lady in my first class that afternoon who was willing to take the steps outside the boundaries despite the fear of falling.

Tamara was one of those girls everyone always liked, and yet no one ever made a big deal about her. She was a sweet, behind-the-scenes kind of girl. One of those people who just has a kind soul and is admired more and more as time passes. Tamara would give me a great gift later that year. Tamara compiled an enormous number of pictures with me in them and put them all together into a photo album. Even though we never hung out much outside of school, Tamara was very much concerned with my happiness. The day I found out I was sick, Tamara could tell I was hurting and simply asked me, "Are you okay?"

How does a person lie to someone who has such genuine concern for one's well-being? I could not and I wanted to share very badly, so I told her, "I found out I have a tumor in my chest."

It was right as the bell was ringing for the next class and she looked at me and said, "I am sorry."

It was after Tamara left another encounter occurred that would change the way I thought about my situation and the way I relayed it to others. As I informed Tamara of my situation, another young man heard what I was saying. He had been a friend of mine for a very long time, but we had not been close lately. He had gone down a different path than I had. Looking back, I feel maybe I could have done more to keep him close to me, but despite the ways in which our lives were headed, he gave me a word of wisdom which I will never forget.

After hearing I was sick, he looked at me and said, "Andrew, I am glad it happened to you." I was taken aback for a second with nothing to say out of astonishment. He realized what I must be thinking and then Terry said these words, "You are strong; I know you will be alright. If it had to happen, I am glad it happened to you."

He was right in ways he might not have known. I was strong. There were so many people who did not have what I had. There were so many people who did not know God, and would not have Him to lean on. I had not been the best man in my adolescent years, but on my knees at night, the voice was just the same as it had been when I was so young and innocent. I think Terry spoke something prophetic into my heart that day. In his words, he relayed to me I was to be strong. I needed to show others why I was strong and it happened to me for a reason. I was moved as I left that conversation, but still very much in need of comfort.

My next class was Calculus and there were two people in that class to whom I very much needed to talk. My two best friends, Blake and Ryan, were in that class, and I knew they would be there for me. As soon as my friends saw me, I knew they could see my heart. I do not know if Blake and Ryan already knew I was sick, but they knew I needed to talk. Blake asked me right away, "You want to go for a walk?"

I responded as I knew I must, "Yes."

Ryan followed as we left and my teacher was more than willing to let us go. We walked out to the football stadium where we had spent so much time together and we just talked. The three of us had been through a lot together. There were girls, or the time when Ryan's house got flooded. Blake's dad had gotten really sick when we were little and had to have a heart transplant. There were so many things we had been through and this was just one more road we had to travel together. I do not even remember what we talked about. It was not the words that were important. I am sure we talked about what was wrong with me, but it was what our hearts said that was much more important.

Those guys loved me and I loved them, too, and as we walked, that bond is what we shared. There was concern, there was hope, and there was fear, but we walked knowing we all shared those emotions and, most of all, we shared a love that was like brothers. In times of great distress, there is something wonderful to be said about an understanding of the heart that does not include words. The understanding I speak of develops over time and experience. It moves us in ways that are not possible without the tears, the blood, and the love that comes with time and trials.

CHAPTER THIRTEEN

The First Cut

§

While David was playing the harp, as he usually did, Saul had a spear in his hand and he hurled it, saying to himself, "I will pin David to the wall." But David eluded him twice. -1 Samuel 18:10-11

I spent little time dwelling on being sick before I was again in a doctor's office. The next day came and I was in Victoria, hoping to get a more detailed diagnosis of what was wrong with me. I endured another CAT scan and found myself again with a lump in my throat waiting to see what it would reveal. Both of my parents were with me at the doctor in Victoria, and it was nice to have them both there. We sat in a rather dim room waiting for the doctor to come in and explain my situation. He finally showed up, and he was a middle-aged man of firm build.

He looked strong at first glance, and as he began to talk he sounded strong as well. He did not speak to me directly at first, but instead addressed my dad. Doctors always addressed Dad first when we were in a room together. I think it is some kind of bond they feel they must establish. I did not understand a lot of what they were talking about at first, until I noticed the change in the doctor's face. He no longer looked strong, but scared. I knew from the look in his eyes it was not going to be a good report.

He began to address me after conversing with my father for a moment. In a voice which was strong, but clearly shaken by the news he had to convey, he said, "Andrew, you have a really large mass in your chest and we have to get it out as soon as possible." It seemed to make sense to me. He continued on, "The mass is cutting off your superior vena cava. It is the vein that drains the blood from your head. It has also pushed your wind pipe off to the side, which is what is causing the trouble breathing."

I quickly went from concerned lump in my throat to really freaking out. I was no doctor, but I was smart enough to know my wind pipe and the vein which drained my head were both rather important parts of my anatomy. I lost the lump just long enough to ask, "What exactly does that mean we have to do?"

The doctor looked at me with the same concerned eyes and replied, "I need to get a sample of the mass in your chest to figure out what needs to be done. We usually do a needle aspiration for this, but your mass is too big."

Later on, Dad would inform me a needle aspiration was when they took a huge needle and shoved it through the chest to get a sample of the tumor. I am really glad I did not know that information when the doctor was talking, or I might have run clear out of the room. The doctor went on to explain I was going to need to have a surgery where a large cut would be made in my chest and a part of the tumor would be removed from my body. The idea of surgery did not sound fun, and I am sure my fear was written all over my face.

The doctor quickly picked up on my nonverbal cue and continued, "Andrew, I know you do not want to do this, but we do not have a choice. Your tumor is about the size of a cantaloupe and if we do not get it out soon your head could start to fill up with blood."

What the doctor said next seemed like the most ridiculous thing in the world at the time, but later I thought it was nice he was considering my situation so personally. I was blown away by the thought of my head filling up with blood. All I could think of were my eyes popping out due to all the pressure from blood in my head. As I sat thinking about my head, the doctor turned to me, adding, "Now, Andrew, you will not be able to do bench press for a while after this surgery."

I thought to myself, *Bench press, who the heck cares about bench press? I think my pecs can suffer a bit to avoid my eyes popping out of my head.*

I did not say anything out loud, but nodded and kept silent. We left the hospital in Victoria with an appointment for surgery with one of the surgeons my dad said was very good. It was starting to dawn on me I was in a lot deeper water than I had first imagined. *They thought that my tumor was the size of a fist yesterday and now it is a cantaloupe?* It hit me hard on the drive home– *I could die.*

I was shaken, but not to the point of tears. I had not really cried over being sick the entire time. I got upset when my parents were upset, but that was not really a cry because I was sick as much as it was a cry because my parents were emotional. I held a firm belief in my heart that kept my tears from flowing. I believed with all my heart God could and would reach into my chest and remove my tumor without a surgery or anything. I thought about what a great witness it would be if the tumor just disappeared. It seemed to me the perfect opportunity for God to show His power and the power of prayer. When I got home, I put that belief into full force as I prayed.

I lay on my bed and looked up to Heaven, crying out for God to hear me, *Father, I know You hear me because You have heard me in the past. Please help me because no one else can, and I need You so much now.* I cried out to God day after day until my surgery. I would visualize a great hand from heaven reaching into my chest and pulling out the tumor. Every time, I would visualize God's hand, and I would call for help. I knew God could answer my prayer and I was sure He would. It seemed like the best thing for everyone if I was miraculously healed.

I look back on those prayers with laughter at how nearsighted I was. I did not have any idea what was going to happen in my life, but I was sure I knew what was best. I was like a child driving a car I did not make, going somewhere I had never been, telling the maker of the car, the one with the map, where to go. I was silly, but I was very sincere. I know now my prayers were heard, it is just some of the bad advice was rightly ignored.

Surgery came quicker than I liked. I had only experienced surgery once before in my life. I recall it was not pleasant for me as I got really sick from the anesthesia I was given and I ended up vomiting for quite some time. I hated to throw up. Apparently there was a whole episode after the last surgery I could not even remember. What I do remember was waking up in the recovery room and feeling wretched. I quickly threw up a few times after I was awake and then my mom was right beside me. She looked at me and said, "Get up, Son, you can throw up at home." My mom is a very practical lady. I blacked out after that only to wake up to a head that looked like it only had one ear. I had to have something removed from behind my ear, and they pressed it down so hard I could not even see it in the mirror.

I also remember screaming really loudly and crying really hard when I first saw myself and thought I would only have one ear forever. What I do *not* remember was how I was apparently laid in my dad's recliner in my parents' bedroom when I first got home. My parents had two recliners, one on each side of a king-sized bed. I was told as soon as I had lain down, I raised back up and projectile vomited all the way across the room, hitting my sister squarely in the face.

I can only sit back and dream about it now, but it must have been amazing: me in a drunken stupor, vomit flying across the room, and my sister sitting in horror in the other recliner. I can hardly imagine how funny it must have been as the missile of vomit nailed her right between the eyes. All the pain and trouble of surgery, and I missed the part where I break the long-distance vomiting record and nail my sister. What a shame.

The day for this second, far more serious surgery finally came and I went under the knife again. This time with the knife was different when I awoke, but no less exciting. Before I went under, I made sure to tell the doctors how sick I had gotten from the anesthesia the last time. I was given some drugs to prevent nausea and they seemed to work well because I did not feel bad at all. I was really groggy, though, and I really needed to go to the bathroom. I quickly realized getting to the bathroom was not a possibility because there was something sticking out of the side of my body and it was attached to a rather large tank.

I did not know what to do so I found a button, pressed it, and muttered something about the bathroom. I was in and out of consciousness for a few minutes until I finally noticed I was standing up. I was still right beside my bed and still connected to the tank, but I was not alone this time. There were two older nurses attending me. They were both holding me under the arms and one was handing me a big jug. I looked at the jug, then at the two nurses, and it occurred to me they wanted me to go to the bathroom in it. I thought about it for a moment and then realized I was too drugged up to care, and went anyway.

As I was standing there in a very medicated state, I understood something. These people did not even know me and they were helping me go to the bathroom. I could not remember anyone helping me pee before, and I was very grateful. I looked at one of the nurses and said, "I love you guys, I think you are both angels." They both smiled and laid me back on my bed, and I was out again.

Those nurses were the first of many examples God would show me of the angelic love people are capable of expressing. I lay in that hospital for three days before I got to go home, and the most extraordinary thing happened to me– people came. My dad stayed in that room more than I thought he should. Dad slept with two small chairs pushed together to stay with me. We both knew he had to go to work every day, but he stayed all night with me until he had to go.

My dad had always loved me, and even though I know it so much better now, it was not as shocking to me as the other people who just stayed for a minute or two. I did not think so many people cared so much about me in my town. I seemed to catch all the bad things people said and never forget them, but the good things people said were always short on my mind. All kinds of friends and all kinds of gifts came by my room in that three-day period.

The trip to the hospital was short, but it came with a range of experiences from great pain to great joy. All those people who came to visit me filled me with a new hope that maybe people cared about me more than I thought they did. The new revelation people brought me was buffered with the pain that brought the realization I still had quite a journey ahead of me. It was right before I left the hospital that I realized how painful things might be in the future. It was physical pain, but I think it spoke to something much deeper than that.

I was told to cut back on the pain medication I was taking a day before I left the hospital. Whenever I was given a request like that, I took it to heart and simply stopped taking the medication. It had been a long time since I had any pain medicine when the doctor came in to remove my chest tube. The long thing sticking out of my side when I had to go to the bathroom was a chest tube. I was glad to hear the tube was going to be out, and I did not think twice about what that would entail. I looked at the doctor and said, "Let's do it."

If I had known what he was about to do, I would have punched him in the face, but I did not. Instead, I just sat there patiently and smiled. My dad grabbed ahold of me, which I thought was weird, and the doctor grabbed the tube in my side and came over with some bandages. In a movement which was not as quick as I would have liked, I felt the doctor pull the tube out of me. It was a sensation that is hard to describe. It felt like he was pulling something out of the very center of my chest and it hurt so bad that it took my breath away. I sat there on the bed with my dad holding me in place and I did not breathe. Dad and the doctor both looked at me and said, "Breathe, Andrew, breathe!"

I looked at them like they were crazy and shook my head back and forth indicating I would not breathe. I could not breathe, and even if I could, I did not want to. I hurt too much. Despite my defiance, I eventually breathed and everybody kind of laughed at me. I do not know what they were laughing about. I would have liked to have seen them after I pulled a tube out of their chest. I eventually recovered from the chest tube extravaganza and we went home. The tumor would have to be sent off to discover what exactly it was.

There was great hope as we left the hospital, however, they were not able to identify the cancer in Victoria because the tumor was so large and much of it was already dead. The good news was many of the doctors thought it was not cancer. We had to wait for the official word from the M.D. Anderson Cancer Center at the University of Texas, but there was hope the tumor was benign.

CHAPTER FOURTEEN

A Tear and a Testimony

§

They mourned and wept and fasted till evening for Saul and his son, Jonathan, and for the army of the Lord and the house of Israel, because they had fallen by the sword. -2 Samuel 1:12

I left the hospital with hope, but I was severely hampered in my physical and emotional states. I did not feel good at all. The surgery was hard on my body. I had already begun to lose weight prior to the surgery, but I was now losing even more and my wounds were significant. The doctor had been very concerned about me not being able to do bench press for a while, and he was quite correct about that restriction. My chest had been butchered and it did not feel in the least bit nice.

There was a large cut about three inches across on my right pec. It was a large cut and I knew it would leave a big scar, but I was not so concerned about the cosmetic appeal. I was more concerned about the fact I felt like my chest was caving in, instead of sticking out. I had bandages all over the right side of my chest, and there was a hole from where the chest tube had been, which that did not feel great either.

I was weak from the surgery and my body felt like it was dying on top of all that had been done to it. It was a hard few days of waiting for the results from M.D. Anderson. My anxiety grew more strenuous when I learned how important the results of the test were going to be. The hard part about being sick when one is a doctor's kid is the whole family knows the gravity of the situation with medical expertise that one would wish never to know. I soon learned if the tumor was benign, I would only require a very large open-chest surgery. The surgery part did not sound good, but in comparison with what I would learn next, it sounded wonderful.

There were apparently five or six different kinds of lymphoma I might have, and all the doctors were sure it was lymphoma if it was cancer. There were good and bad elements regarding the different kinds of lymphoma I might have. The good element was there was one kind of cancer, Hodgkin's disease, which had a great success rate. The bad news was if I got any of the other kinds of cancer, the likelihood I would die quickly became almost certain. My mass was so large that if they did not stop it as soon as possible, I would be in a great deal of trouble. I was overwhelmed by the possibilities that awaited me.

There was nothing physically I could do to help my situation. Up until this point in my life, I was always sure I could work my way out of things. If I was not doing well in sports, I would work harder. If I could not get the girl I wanted, I would pursue harder. If I did not get the grades I wanted, I would study harder. It seemed a natural progression of life that one could make oneself into whatever was desired. I sat in my house with nothing I could do harder. What could I do harder? I could not "live" harder, that was not possible. No, there was nothing I could do better in this world that would help. I sat lingering in the anxiety of feeling helpless and alone. The hope I had felt for my sickness was now being overwhelmed by fear of what might lay ahead of me.

There is only one true antidote within human recourse to relieve stress and fear, and that is prayer. I realized there was nothing I could do harder but pray. My hope was only that God would intervene, and so I went to the one place in which my soul felt the most open and honest in the day time. At night, that place was my bed, but during the day the place in which my prayer life became the most real and the most vulnerable was the bathtub. I do not know if it was because I was physically naked in to the bathtub that I felt the most vulnerable and open to God or not, but that is where I felt it.

The bathtub was a place where my soul could open up and be free of all the restrictions life seemed to place on a young man's emotions. No one would see me cry in the bath and no one would hear my conversation. It was a sanctuary of the strangest kind and yet it soothed my soul in ways my limited writing ability will not do justice.

I had a regular pattern of bath prayer in my parents' house. I would surround myself by what was familiar and comforting. Before I went to the tub, I would always get a glass of Dr. Pepper. Dr. Pepper was the drink on which I grew up. My grandfather drank Dr. Pepper when I would go to visit him. Grandpa would always have these clear, small glasses that seemed just right for my hand and just small enough so the drink would always stay really cold and not become watered down when I drank it.

I loved those summers I spent with my grandparents and the Dr. Pepper reminded me of them. It also reminded me of my dad, who had been giving me Dr. Pepper in containers as far back as bottles. It was my favorite drink, and it was my comfort drink. I would go to the kitchen and fill up a glass. It could not be any glass it had to be a certain kind. I was a lot bigger than I had been with my grandpa and there was a new kind of glass that was my favorite. I would find it and fill it up. It was a plastic glass with a mug-like handle. It was not too big, but not really small either, so I knew it would last through the bath.

After attaining the Dr. Pepper, I would go to the only bathroom in the house that would do for such a serious time of prayer. My parents' bathroom was by far my favorite. It was huge and the bathtub was amazing. It was one of those tubs that has the stairs incasing it. It was big enough to submerge my whole body in water all at one time if that was what I wanted to do. When I was little, I would always fill it up as much as possible. I did not really like all the extra water, I just wanted the hot water to continue to fill the tub. There was something about the hot water still coming out I really liked.

Possibly the best part of the tub was the armrests. There were arm rests on both sides of the tub which were perfect for relaxing since the edges of the tub were much too high for a person's arms. The tub was a Jacuzzi tub, but the jets did not concern me. It would have ruined the whole experience to have some really loud jets running while I was trying to talk with God.

I soon found myself submerged in everything I thought wonderful, and as the bath water poured out, I poured out my soul. I had not really cried about what was happening to me until that day. It had all come crashing down on me so fast and the reality of it was squeezing my heart with ferocity. The assurance that was so strong earlier began to give way.

I began to pray as I did earlier. I was envisioning God reaching into my chest and pulling out the mess that lay within me. My heart was sinking as I cried out, "God why have You not answered my prayer? I know You hear me and I know You can heal me. Please pull the tumor out!"

It was growing inside of me, but I did not want to admit it. People of faith did not think those kinds of thoughts. I could not think that either! I had my problems with sin, but I loved God and I believed in Him deeply. I would not think it! I tried all I could to keep it from coming out, but I finally could not hold it in any longer. I burst forth, "I do not want to die!"

Tears began to flow down my face as I said it. I do not know what the tears were for exactly. They may have been because I was afraid of dying, or they may have been because I was so sad I had to say I was scared of dying. Deep in my heart, I thought I should not be scared, but I was really scared and I could not lie to God or myself any longer.

There was not much to say after I let that confession out. I think I was drawn into prayer just to admit it. It was as if I needed to admit to God I was scared and I needed to cry with Him. He let me cry and He sat there with me. He did not really say anything, but as I cried I could feel Him all around me. He was in the warm water that comforted me and in the drink that reminded me of safety. He was in all those things I loved so much, and yet it was deeper than that. I cried and He sat inside me and held my heart in His hands. It is the same feeling a person gets when he is young and is cold so his mom wraps a blanket around him to keep him warm. I cried for the first time and He did not leave me. He let me cry and wrapped my heart in comfort.

It may be when we cry God can use us the most. It is as if God catches our tears and uses them to water the souls of our fellow men. The tears of believers are a refreshing shower to those over whom they are poured. It is not the tears themselves that are refreshing, but the growth they bring. Tears remind us of each other's humanity. A weak people born with fragile hearts try so often to look strong and tears bring down every illusion. In the truthfulness of a saint's tears comes another blessing. When a heart falls low, God has a great opportunity to lift it up for the world to see and be encouraged.

I was hurting as I waited to find out my test results, but I had not forgotten what my friend, Terry, had said to me that day in school about my strength, and what God had said through Terry. I wanted to share with the world Jesus Christ was the reason I would survive. He was the reason for everything and I had long tried to hide my love of Him. I could not hide it any longer and I wanted a chance to shout out all I felt in such a weak and revealing state. Maybe there was something I could share with the world. When it is for the right reasons, and one desires to share the love of the Lord with the people the Lord loves, God always provides the opportunity to speak. He never fails to do so, although sometimes it is in ways that are different than anyone thought possible.

It was during a time when I wanted to share that Mike Foresight called for me. Mike was the sports writer for the local Victoria paper. Mike and I had met before and we were friendly acquaintances. Mike had done a really nice story on me my sophomore year of football as we made our run to State. Mike had covered a great number of my games and knew as much about my sports career as anyone. Mr. Foresight wanted to do an interview with me about my sickness. I was excited when he called and thought it was a great chance to do some good with the situation in which I found myself. Mr. Foresight showed up one afternoon and as I sat in my living room, we talked and God worked.

There was a great article written in the Victoria paper about me. I have to give credit to Mr. Foresight because he made me sound a lot better than I think I actually was. He spoke about me and my situation and he wrote about my faith. There were many things said in that article, and I am not sure what about it touched people, but I truly believe it did. I had not done anything spectacular except get sick, but God was starting to use it to inspire people.

The article reached people all around my area and they got to hear about my reason for hope. Jesus was in that article and that truth was what was most important to me. All the people who knew me from sports soon got to hear about my faith, but it was what happened later with the article that blew me away. It did not just stop with my area, the article was placed on the A.P. wire and was sent all over the place. I had a friend call me from Dallas, Texas and tell me it appeared in their newspaper. God was using my situation to touch people from all over the place and He was going to use the people to touch me.

CHAPTER FIFTEEN

Little Angels

§

While David was at Horesh in the Desert of Ziph, he learned Saul had come out to take his life. And Saul's son Jonathan went to David at Horesh and helped him find strength in God. -1 Samuel 23:15-16

Why is forgiveness so hard? It is very easy to say one is sorry, but to truly forgive someone is one of the hardest things to do in life. It is especially hard to forgive when there is no one person who bears the wrath of one's anger. It is even more astounding that forgiveness is so hard for Christians. We all know Christians who hold the longest, most hateful grudges of anyone we know. How is it the people who are forgiven so much are unable to forgive so little? In my own life, I have come to only one conclusion. I struggle with forgiveness when I do not truly feel God has forgiven me. There is no other explanation that can be true, because if

I could grasp even a hint of what God's forgiveness means, I would have no choice but to forgive others. The joy that comes with being released of a great debt must cause the charity of the heart to increase in abundance.

I still harbored resentment in my heart for people in general as I waited for the results of my test. I was not dwelling on how I felt about society, but it was in the back of my mind. I had not forgotten the harsh words of people after football games. They seemed to be stamped on the back of my brain and I was not willing to let them go. It was still me against the world. I could see life no other way. I thought God was on my side, as if He was not on everyone else's side as well. I would attribute this selfish paradigm to my teenage years, except I do not believe that selfishness it is a quality of teenagers only. If it were not for the events that followed that changed my heart, I am sure I would still have a completely self-absorbed mindset.

It was not long until I found myself in the car headed to Houston. My dad's connections in the medical world had allowed me to be fast-tracked through the system at M.D. Anderson. I was having my test reviewed by a friend of my dad's in the leukemia ward of the hospital. I am at somewhat of a loss as to how to describe the car ride to Houston. It is about three and a half hours from my house to the hospital there. It is hard to describe the feeling that came as I rode in the car to a place where I would learn if I would live or die.

There would be no absolute certainty in the test results, but there were great probabilities of my death with
certain outcomes of the tests. I was decidedly certain the
tumor would not be malignant while my mom and dad
were both desperately hoping it was Hodgkin's disease.
Dad seemed pretty sure it was Hodgkin's disease and did
not give me any hope it would be benign.

I made it through the first ten minutes of the car ride
just fine, but I am quite sure they were the longest ten
minutes of my life. The weight of that car ride was so
thick I could taste it. No one was excited and I could tell
everyone was really scared. It is a funny feeling when
everyone is clearly terrified and yet everyone is trying to
pretend everything is alright.

We were not even to Victoria when my dad told me
he had something to give me. He turned to my mother in
the back seat and asked her to hand me the box which sat
beside her. She handed me a medium-sized box with no
real distinguishing marks on it. The box clearly was not a
present from a shop. I looked at the box wondering what
it was and my dad turned to me and said, "It was given to
me by one of the nurses who lives in Yoakum." I started
to open the box and as I did, I soon found it was not a
present from a store, but something much better.

As I opened the box, letters started to pour out onto
my lap. They were not fancy letters done with calligra-
phy and personalized envelopes, they were something
much more meaningful. They were letters done with
crayons and person ally decorated with hand-drawn pic-

tures. As I began to read the letters, I started to cry. I could not stop crying. It was not a cry that comes after a sad movie or the tears that come when one gets physically hurt. There was something in my soul that broke and there was a torrential flood that followed. I cried and I just kept reading. There were hundreds of letters in that box and they were all from children at a private school in Yoakum. Yoakum was our biggest rival in football and only fifteen minutes from our town. The letters all looked fairly similar in format, but they were extraordinary individual messages that pierced my heart.

The letters all said things like, "Andrew, even though you are from Cuero you are my favorite quarterback," or "I am praying for you, Andrew, and I know God will help you," or "Be strong, Andrew, God loves you!" I think most of the cards were written by children under 10-years-old, and it was the most beautiful poetry I had ever read. The cards were decorated with pictures of football players and crosses. Each card seemed to be done with such genuine care by such small fingers.

I am swelling up with tears just thinking about it so many years later. The things those kids wrote in their cards showed me a love I had not known before. I might have experienced love in this capacity at some point in the past, but it was not until I was completely broken and God brought those cards to me that I realized it. At the bottom of every card there were little names written in handwriting that resembled someone writing with their non-dominant hand. At the bottom of every letter, there was a name of a little angel who blessed my life.

The blessing did not stop with the cards of those kids. When the Lord decides to bless a person's life, that person had better bring a raincoat because it will rain like monsoon season. I was handed more cards from all kinds of people. There were cards from kids at high schools we played sports against. So many people wrote prayers and encouraging words to me. There was a huge banner that was signed by all my classmates with words of encouragement and prayers for me. The world I believed so much to be against me was coming into my corner with full force in the time when I needed help most. Love was gushed over my proud, resentful heart, and under so much weight, my heart broke.

The range of emotions that ensued would change the rest of my life. I was desperately sorry for how I had felt about people in general. I had been hard-hearted and ignored so many people because of the so very few who had been mean to me. There was a whole world of people who obviously loved me more than I had thought possible and it had taken until I was about to die for me to realize their love. I knew right then and there how I very much did *not* want to die. The love God had shown me through the love of His people caused me desperately not to want to leave this world. There were so many things to do and so many people to love and I had just realized it. The veracity with which I wanted to live gripped my heart stronger than it had ever hit me before.

My parents tried to console me as I wept. Through my tears I was saying, "I do not want to die. I do not want to die." My parents were trying to tell me I was not going to die, but I am not sure I was talking to them. There was a subtle shift starting to happen in my soul, because before that day I wanted to do good things for people, but only because I wanted to do good things for God. I knew God loved people, but that was His prerogative, and I found it had little to do with me. I may not have ever said this previous viewpoint out loud, because I knew all the appropriate Sunday school answers, but in my heart that is exactly how I felt. That day, in the midst of so many letters, God used people to show me love. I rode in a car to find out if I was going to die, and what I found out was not only did I love God, but I loved His people, too.

I am fully convinced God's hand is among us. I am also convinced often we miss the hand of God because it looks too much like our own. Were those children angels? They did not have wings, but I know they were messengers from God. Every crayon was marked by a divine seal. They were small and looked a lot like me, but that day they flew out into my desert and ministered to me. In a car on Highway 59 in Texas, manna was dropped from heaven and it came in the form of letters colored with crayons. I had never tasted anything so sweet.

CHAPTER SIXTEEN

The Diagnosis

§

Yet as surely as the Lord lives and as you live, there is only one step between me and death. -1 Samuel 20:3

It was not long before we arrived in Houston. As we pulled into the medical complex, I was overwhelmed by my surroundings. The M.D. Anderson Medical Center was enormous. We pulled into the circle drive at the front of the building and both the size of the building and the expectations of what awaited me inside were bigger than anything I had previously experienced. We made our way into the lobby, where a mountain of paperwork awaited us. It seemed forever before we were done checking in. Every piece of paper we had to fill out was like another thorn in my side. The stress was piercing my flesh and affecting my stomach. I felt horribly nauseous as we went through all the hoops of a big medical facility.

I had been feeling nauseous quite a bit, but this feeling was more excruciating than usual.

We finally made it through the paperwork and headed upstairs to the leukemia ward of the hospital. I knew I did not have leukemia, but my dad's friend who worked in that department was going to tell me what I did have. I will never forget the faces I found upstairs in that hospital. I pray I will never forget how my heart broke.

The hospital waiting room was large and filled with the uncomfortable chairs that are entirely too close to people whom one has never met. I am not sure if those chairs would be comfortable even if they were La-Z-Boys®. We found a group of chairs in the back corner and sat down. I lowered myself onto my chair, hoping I might be able to fall asleep. I wanted so much to fall asleep. I wanted to close my eyes so I did not have to see everything that was in front of me. I so badly wanted to hide, but there was nowhere to hide. The stark reality of life was hitting me in the face and there was nowhere to run.

It is a hard question every man who desires to be great, or sometimes just to survive, must answer. Can he endure the good with the bad? Is he able to look at that which is most horrible in life and say, "I will not wilt under the heat of adversity"? I believe there are great men who look at that which is so painful and say, "I will learn and I will help." I truly believe there are a few men in life who stand at the frontlines of battle and say, "I will not run, even while they shoot."

I was not one of those men. I was, and am, an ordinary man who was scared out of his mind, but was forced to stand anyway. For those of us who are forced to stand and watch the terror we would otherwise run away from, it is a learning experience that changes us forever. The heart of a man is never the same after he is forced to stand and watch his fellow man die. There are some who are forced to stand and yet refuse to watch. Some people see the horrors of life and convince themselves they never really happened. To those poor, miserable few, I pray they would open their eyes, for the state of their heart is at risk.

I looked up from my seat in that waiting room and saw the other people waiting in their chairs. They were people who had families, people who loved and were loved. Many were frightened for their lives just as I was, and it was written all over their bodies. Others were only shells of what must have been a vibrant former self. I walked the halls of a proverbial concentration camp from the seat of my hospital chair. The hurt in that hospital was not incurred by Nazis, but by a world with evil running freely through it. When I looked into the faces of my fellow patients, I knew I lived in a hard world where people were in need of great help.

I looked across the room and saw a woman. I do not know how old she was. There was no way of telling because of the toll sickness had taken on her body. Her cheek bones seemed so large, but only because her face was so gaunt from her body eating her alive. Her eyes were dark and sunk back into her head, but there was still a sparkle of hope found within them. She had not given up yet, but it looked as if she was on the verge of giving up. I think the saddest thing for me was her hair. She really did not have any hair at all, and the little that was left was covered up by a bandana. There is something so sad to me, as a young man, when I see a woman who has lost her hair. A woman's hair is so beautiful and covers her like a garment no man could make. This poor lady had been stripped down and ravaged by disease. There were all sorts of I.V.s coming out of her, and as I looked on I was ripped into pieces.

I turned away as quickly as I could. I could not watch anymore. It was as if something was eating her and I could feel it eating me, too. I was terrified and so sad. As I turned away, I noticed there were people all over that room who looked just like she did. There was nowhere my eyes could turn to escape the hurt. Everywhere I looked people were suffering and soon I felt deep within me I would suffer, too.

It is interesting how sympathy and understanding work. A man never cares deeply for people the way he is capable of feeling for them until he feels pain will happen to him soon or when painful things are happening to him. It is as if pain is not really pain unless it happens directly to us. Pain is rampant in our world and it does not matter if we sit on our leather couches in the suburbs or in a tent in the Mojave Desert, people suffer.

I did not want to see it. If I could just avoid seeing it, then it was not really happening. I could not avoid seeing it, however, or the reality that it was truly happening. I wanted to curl up in a ball. I wanted to cry. I wanted to run away, but there was nowhere to run to and there was only one thing I could do. I had to watch and I had to learn. I did not grasp it all at once, but I was learning the hardest lesson men face in our world: I was learning I was not the only one living. I was learning I was not the only one hurting.

It sounds like such an obvious thing to have to learn. Obviously there are people all around us, but do we really know they are there? There are different kinds of knowledge, and the kind I was experiencing was of an experiential nature which settles into the very soul of a man. To know people suffer is much different than knowing their suffering. To know people live is much different than living with people. True lives are not lived in bubbles. True lives are lived through the sloshing and intermixing of souls and lives. I say sloshing because our lives are fluid. Humanity is an ever-changing experience in which we should hold each other's hands, but we are afraid. I was afraid if I experienced, if I saw the hurt in other people's lives, then the hurt in my own life would be more real.

The reason people like the bubbles of life so much comes from the fact the reflection from within their bubble keeps them from seeing out of it. If one never sees the hurt in other people, one does not notice the gradual destruction of one's own life. The thing about very slow change is that it is hard to notice any difference until the changing is done. A person in a bubble stares at themselves every day thinking he or she does not look much different than the day before. One can trick oneself into avoiding noticing the deterioration of one's soul this way. It is an awful trick we play on ourselves. Yet, sometimes, the Lord pops someone's bubble so he can see those around him. It then becomes the job of the freed man to pop the bubbles of his fellow man.

I sat looking at the horror that surrounded me and began to realize I could stare at my reflection within my own bubble no longer. God showed me a love from people on the way to the hospital and inside the hospital God showed me how much those people needed help.

I began to become more comfortable with the look of the people who surrounded me in the waiting room, but I also began to become distressed by something else. Remember, I really did not care for needles, and as I sat in the waiting room, I began to realize where everyone was going. There were a few people who went into rooms that looked like offices, but most of the people were headed into a room that scared the daylights out of me. As I watched patient after patient leave the room, I noticed they all went under the same sign and into the same room.

There was a large door with a sign over the top that said something about injections. I am not sure what the rest of the sign said, because I was too scared to read past the word *injection*. I was scared enough of shots, but there was some-thing worse I had heard about, and the thought of it was distressing me to the point of shaking. I had heard my dad talk about a bone marrow examination. I did not really understand what all was involved in the examination, but it involved a big needle and that was all I needed to know to be really scared. People came and people left and the horror did not stop until finally someone called my name, "Andrew Heard."

I found myself walking into the back of a long corridor. I did not want to walk, but my legs were moving and my parents were behind me, so I could not stop. I was about to find out what was wrong with me. We entered an examination room and we were asked to take a seat. We did and we waited. As we waited, I was scared, so I talked. "I know it is going to be benign," I said as I looked at the posters on the wall.

There are always very strange things on the walls in doctor's offices. There are picture of the inside of bodies and pictures of horrible infections and diseases. All the pictures have very convenient explanations of what is wrong with the picture. I think doctors are crazy! Why would they think the first thing I want to see when I walk into a room where I will find out how deathly sick I am is a picture of some nasty fungus I could get, or that every sick patient wants to know all the disgusting details of the inner workings of their malfunctioning bodies? What are people thinking?

I was not overly troubled by the pictures I looked at as I waited because I had seen all the same type of pictures in my dad's offices my whole life. After a few minutes of my parents talking to me, the doctor finally showed up. At least I thought he was the doctor, until he opened his mouth. He was an intern and he was coming in to pre-inform us of the situation. I did not care if he was Doctor Seuss, as long as he told me what was wrong with me.

The intern sat down on his little swiveling chair and began to look at a chart, and as he did he turned to me and said, "Well, it looks like you could have one of three kinds of leukemia."

My eyes got big as I turned and looked at him. "Leukemia?!" I said in a frantic voice. I knew enough about leukemia from the waiting room to know I did not want anything to do with leukemia. I looked back at my dad with a *please save me* look on my face. Surely this intern did not know what he was talking about. No one had thought I had leukemia.

Dad quickly tried to intervene and told the intern, "I do not believe he could have leukemia. We are just here to find out the test results because I know the doctor." The intern did not know my dad was a doctor and looked at him with a funny expression.

The intern turned and said, "Well, I did not know about that, but I will send the doctor in as soon as possible." The intern left, not realizing he had devastated me beyond belief. I sat in the chair for the next few minutes scared out of my mind I had leukemia. Dad tried to reassure me I did not have leukemia, but here I was, hoping I did not have cancer, and now someone thought I had leukemia. I knew how big my tumor was and I knew what leukemia could do to me.

I was so upset I had nothing to say. I was waiting for the doctor when I began to realize something that struck terror into my heart– I might have to have a bone-marrow biopsy if I had cancer. It seems like a silly thing to worry about, but that needle was hovering over me like a lion ready to strike. I could almost feel the pain ripping through my body as I waited for the doctor.

The doctor finally made his way to our room, and as he entered I jumped at the chance to talk to him. I quickly informed him the intern had told us I had some form of leukemia. He could tell I was upset and, looking a little annoyed, he turned to me and said, "No, you do not have leukemia." I was relieved and hope started to reinvade my mind.

Maybe it is benign, I thought as the doctor turned toward the direction of my dad.

My hope quickly faded as the doctor looked at my father and said, "I am afraid I do have some bad news."

"Bad news" was not a phrase I wanted to hear and as the doctor spoke, my mind began to race, *I do not have cancer! It has to be benign! This is not happening to me!* I wanted to think I was not hearing what I was hearing, but there was no way of stopping it and eventually I had to face it.

The doctor finally turned and addressed me, asking, "Do you understand what I am saying, Andrew?"

Sure, I knew what he was saying. I had heard the entire conversation, I just did not want to believe it. My mind raced for some way to get out of having to believe what the doctor was saying was true, but there was no way out. I had to face what he was trying to tell me, and so I asked the most important question I could think of, "Will I have to have a bone-marrow biopsy?" Maybe it was not the most grown-up question I could ask, but it seemed pretty important to me at the time.

Looking a little surprised at the question, the doctor drew back and said, "Well, yes, Son, you will."

I drew back within myself at the answer. I was so scared at the information that had just passed through that room. All the things I wanted most to avoid were all coming into reality. I felt like the kid who does not want to be called on in class because he did not do his homework. He sits and hopes the teacher will not call on him so everyone will not know he is not prepared to answer. If there was ever a time when I was not prepared to answer, this was it. There was now a question hanging in the air and it was addressed directly to me: "Will you survive cancer?"

It turned out my dad was right. I had Hodgkin's disease and I had a major case of it. If I was going to get cancer this was the one to get, but I sure did not want to have cancer. At all. I knew people who had Hodgkin's disease in the past and I knew some of their treatments were not all that bad, so I was hopeful with a little radiation I would be out of the rough waters.

The doctor who told me the results of my test referred us to another physician. The doctor was very nice as we left him. He looked at me and said, "Andrew, Dr. Hart," who was the doctor I was going to see, "is the world's foremost expert on Hodgkin's disease. He will take care of you. Oh, and I will make sure you have the easiest time possible with the bone-marrow biopsy."

It was nice to hear him be so supportive, but knowing he was not the one facing the needle, I did not feel as great as he was trying to make it sound. I left his office a little scared, but not overly frightened. It was the best answer I could have gotten for having cancer. I knew I had a good chance and my parents were as happy as one could expect in such a situation, all of which helped my attitude a lot.

CHAPTER SEVENTEEN

The Pit and the Rope that Pulls Us Out

§

A messenger came and told David, "The hearts of the men of Israel are with Absalom." -2 Samuel 15:13

It seems we walk quite a long path in our lives. The path would be really enjoyable if it were not for all the uphill walking and pits into which we fall. I have often found myself to be blind even though my eyes work perfectly well. I am blind in knowing what is ahead of me in life. I walk along the path of life, and sometimes there are no bumps in the road, but other times I find there seems to be no road at all. I walk the path that has been laid before me, and I never see the fall coming. One step, everything appears to be just fine. The next step, I find myself falling into a pit I cannot climb out of on my own. I try furiously to walk up the side of that pit, but I make no ground. The more I try and struggle to climb out, the dirtier I get. I do not make it out of the pit, I only cover myself in mud. It is there, on the bottom of the muddy floor, I finally sit down. I stop moving and look at where I am. Many times, I have to take a moment to move all the mud from my eyes so I can see. Then, when my eyes are clean, I take a look at the hole into which I have fallen.

I realize all my frantic attempts to climb out have only made my situation worse. It is when I have taken the time to put aside the crazed anxiety, which I think will save me, I see there is a way out. Looking as though it has been there the entire time, I find a rope. When the world seems to fall beneath one's feet, look around in wonder. For it is on the ride out of the hole that one experiences the touch of divinely made fingers. It is the man who lets the circumstances of the hole run away with his mind who misses the joy of being saved. There is always a rope, but some men have to have it tied to their bodies while other men just grab ahold.

***

We arrived in Dr. Hart's office and I was not terribly anxious except for the reoccurring thoughts of needles plaguing my mind. After what cannot be described as a brief wait, we were taken to one of the examination rooms to wait to meet the doctor. Dr. Hart entered our exam room and was not at all the type of person I expected him to be. I do not know what I thought the world's expert on Hodgkin's disease would look like, but he was not it.

He was sharper looking than I thought he would be. I was expecting a rather old man with a funny beard and glasses. I thought he might be wearing a lab coat with a funny bowtie. Instead of a funny bowtie, Dr. Hart had on a very nice tie I thought looked uncannily in style. He was also not as old as I thought he would be, and was clean-shaven.

He looked stylish, but what he had to say was not as palatable as his dress. He was clearly all business as he entered the room. He greeted us with a smile I knew was forced, a reoccurring social obligation which he was required to perform. Dr. Hart had serious business he had to discuss and it was clear from his expression that was what he was about.

He went about the normal first-time visit rituals. He asked me about my symptoms and what had been done so far. I repeated the same things which I had told all the doctors before him. After a fairly uneventful examination, Dr. Hart sat down in a chair in the opposite corner of the room from me and started to write in a chart. As he wrote he began to talk, and the topic of his conversation pulled the ground out from under me.

I had gotten a little nervous from his serious demeanor during the examination, but I was trying to be strong. Dr. Hart looked up at my dad as he spoke. "Well, we have a stage four occurrence of Hodgkin's disease. There are a couple of treatment options we can look at. There is the normal regiment of six months of chemotherapy and two months of radiation I prescribe, or there is an advanced, heavy treatment which is condensed into a shorter time period."

My eyes started to water and my heart started to hurt as I heard the doctor say the word *chemotherapy*. I did not know exactly what all was involved in chemotherapy, but I had seen some people who were close to me waste away into nothing on chemotherapy. I realized the treatment the doctor was describing was really serious. The doctor looked very grave and there was something not as comforting in his talk as when my dad spoke about my sickness. I wanted to act tough, but I could feel myself becoming weak. I wanted to curl up in the fetal position and cry.

The doctor and my dad continued to talk about medicines and things I did not understand. I could not stop thinking about chemotherapy and six months. Six months was a really long time. The gravity of my situation was becoming greater with every moment. I wished it was all a bad dream. As I daydreamed and tried to hold back tears, I overheard my dad say he thought the six-month treatment would be better. The success rate on the six-month regiment was good and it had a lot lower rate of developing other cancers later in life. I did not know what to say when they looked to me for approval so I just said, "Yes, I agree."

After deciding how to proceed with treatment, the doctor sat down and explained we would have to stay at the hospital for a number of days to go through a series of test. I really did not want to have any more tests done, because it seemed like only bad news came with tests and I wanted to go home. Despite my wishes, there did not seem to be a way out of it, so I just sat there on the examination table. There was finally a pause in the conversation and I took the chance to speak up. I wanted desperately to ask a question. It was hard to talk as I tried to ask it. There was a burning sensation that went all the way down the back of my throat and it seemed as if my throat was only big enough let get air in, but not out of it. I did not think anything would come out as I tried to talk.

In a shaky voice, I finally spoke up. "Dr. Hart?" I hoped so much that his answer would be yes, "Will I be alright?" My voice shook even harder when I finally said it. I did not want to cry, especially in front of a grown man I did not know, but I could not help it. Tears started to run down my face as I looked at him, waiting for an answer. Surely he would say yes. Dr. Hart was an honest man and as he turned to me I could see that I was going to get an honest answer.

He looked at me and said, "Andrew, I cannot promise you anything."

I was so scared! *The doctor does not know if I will be alright.*

Knowing I needed more than that response, Dr. Hart continued, "Most of my patients do very well and there is a high probability you will, too. You do have a very large mass, but Hodgkin's disease is very treatable in today's world. You will be alright." I was not at all reassured by the doctor's response and I left that examination room feeling like I had fallen into the biggest pit of my life, and I was sure I would never make it out.

The most excruciating part of that day was how it seemed I continued to fall onto sharper and sharper objects. I went straight from the examination room to another waiting room. As I sat in the waiting room, I was horrified at the awful things that awaited me in that hospital. I had not even been in the hospital twenty-four hours and it was already my least favorite place on Earth. There was a stench of sterilization that suffocated me with every breath. When the world seems all black, even the things which would be considered wonderful take on a wretched connotation.

There was a group of volunteers in the hospital who went from waiting room to waiting room to hand out tea and coffee, trying to help the patients as much as possible. They were the sweetest old ladies anyone could encounter, and yet as I stared at them on that very dark day, all I could see them with was contempt. *Why would someone spend any time in such a wretched place?* My thoughts were covered with the mud that comes as one strives to climb out of a pit on one's own. I am ashamed I thought such things about people with obviously wonderful hearts.

My thoughts did not occupy me long before my mother pulled out a piece of paper she had received from the doctor. She said, "I got a list of your scheduled appointments." I stared at her with a look of disgust and waited for the next bit of terrible news to come my way. Mom looked at me with sad eyes and continued, "You have a bone-marrow biopsy next." I was mad at the world when she told me what my next appointment was. As soon as I learned what was ahead of me, my anger turned to fear. I sat quietly in my chair, feeling very alone as I waited for my name to be called.

The best way I can describe the gravity of the situation is to describe an encounter I had in the waiting room. There was a man sitting just across from my parents and me as we waited to get the procedure done. The man was in his forties and he was with his wife. He did not say much as we sat there, but his wife was rather talkative. She was telling my mom about where they were from and what they did for a living. The husband just sat there with a disturbed look on his face as we waited. I noticed right away he was the one who was sick. I could always tell who was sick and who was not because all the patients were required to wear wristbands on their arms.

As my mom talked with his wife, a lady came out into the corridor and called out a name. I did not know the name, but I soon found out to whom it belonged. The man across from me burst into tears at the sound of his name. I was not accustomed to seeing a grown man cry, and as he did, I was shocked and scared. I did not understand why the man was crying, but I rationalized it must be because of something bad. The man finally composed himself and went back with the lady calling his name. After the man had left, his wife turned to my mother and said, "I am sorry about all that. My poor husband cries every time he has to have his bone-marrow biopsy done."

I could not believe a grown man would cry like that over a procedure and I asked my dad about it. Dad looked at me calmly and said, "Well, the procedure is painful and it very much depends on who is doing it as to how much it hurts."

I sat in despair as I heard someone say my name. There was a woman's voice from the far side of the room. The waiting room was a long, hallway-like room, with one side covered with windows and the other side containing a series of random openings. These openings were corridors to the different section of the hospital. There, in the middle corridor, was a voice calling, "Andrew Heard."

My name was something I used to love to hear other people say. However, in the recent days, my name had become something I loathed to hear. With every syllable of my name, I expected something bad to happen. The woman who called my name was a rather nice-looking lady. She was obviously a mother and had rosy cheeks that kind of cheered me up just looking at them. The woman had on medical scrubs and she waited for me with a chart in her hand.

I got up from my seat and headed for her. She introduced herself and said she would be performing my biopsy. I tried to be nice and smile, but it was clear from my expression I was very scared and I had no desire to follow her down the hall. The woman could tell I was nervous and she was making every effort to comfort me. It was not the kind of coddling that comes when someone is just trying to do what they feel obligated to do. As the lady spoke to me, I could tell she obviously really cared I was not too frightened. Looking at me with very warm eyes, she said, "Andrew, I have heard you are a little nervous about this procedure."

I thought to myself, *I am not just nervous, I am terrified.* I did not want to sound like a wimp so I just replied, "Yes, ma'am."

Looking as if she understood me more than I did myself she said, "Well, do not worry. I will walk you through the whole thing." It was not what she said that made me feel better, but it was somehow the way in which she said it. People can say things from their heart and one knows right away it is genuine. I do not know how one knows, but there is no denying it. Her heart sympathized with me as we walked down that hall. It was as if her heart reached out to mine and bore the pain with me.

We came to the door of the exam room, and as we opened it I felt as though all my fears were about to be realized. If anyone is wondering why a young man would be so afraid of a needle, I think I should take a moment to explain the bone-marrow biopsy procedure. It is true I was a little fearful of normal needles, but the needle I was about to encounter was not just any needle.

A bone-marrow biopsy is a difficult process. There has to be an extraction of the marrow inside of one's bones. In order to do this, the needle must puncture the bone to aspirate the fluid. As one can imagine, breaking through bone with a needle is a pretty hard process. There is no way to fully numb the bone and therefore the person must just grit their teeth as the needle is pushed through it. For the needle not to break, an extremely large and very sturdy needle is used. In my opinion, they should change the name from *needle* to *metal straw*, because that name is a more accurate description.

The exam room had a table in it and the table had two stirrups at the front end. As we came into the room the woman with me began to explain the procedure. She sat me down and in a kind voice told me, "Okay, Andrew, we are going to have to make two extractions off both sides of your pelvic bone. What I am going to have you do is lie down on the exam table, belly down. Then I will numb your bone up as much as I can before we push with the big needle. Once you are numb, I will make a couple of big pushes on the needle and we will be done. After we get through with both sides, it will all be over."

I got up from the seat and got onto the exam table. The woman doing my procedure had a great comforting effect on me and I got the courage to grip the stirrups in front of the table. I had decided I could make it through and I would just grab those stirrups as hard as I could until it was over. As we got ready for the procedure, the lady made every effort to get me to loosen up. We talked about what I liked to do and what sports I played. She had a son who was about my age.

As she began to numb me with the smaller needles, she even commented on my boxers, saying that her son had the same pair. I laughed because an older woman was looking at my boxers. She was making me laugh when all I wanted to do before I came in was cry. She was amazing. The numbing was soon over and she was about to stick the big needle in me. The numbing had gone really well and I was scared as she told me what she was about to do, but not nearly as much as I thought I would be. I gripped the stirrups in front of me with everything I had. I was going to tear those stirrups off if I could. Then with unexpected force, the woman jumped on the needle she had placed in my back.

A sharp whip of pain shot through my body. I clenched my teeth and then it was over. It was not that bad! Oh, it hurt, but I was alive and had survived. The woman quickly asked if I was okay. I said, "Yes."

With a relived breath she said, "Good, one more to go."

The next stick on the opposite side of my back was a breeze. Well, as much as having a straw crammed through one's back can be a breeze. I could not believe how little it had hurt. I wanted to hug the lady. My eyes were teary because of the pain and because I had been so very scared. I was bandaged up and, after carefully putting my cloths back on, I turned and faced the woman who had been so kind to me. She was smiling and said, "Well, you made it through." She was right. I had made it through with a great deal of help from her. There are times in life when we need ropes. There are even times in life when we need a hand finding the rope that is waiting to pull us out of our hole. That day among needles and pain, a wonderful woman at M.D. Anderson was my rope.

As I left the room that had caused me so much anxiety, I waddled more than I could walk. I was a little hobbled by the biopsy, but my spirit was greatly improved. The people God uses to pull his children out of the pits of life can be so unexpected and yet so wonderful. I was leaving as the woman called to me, "Andrew, I have something I want to give you." I looked at her with curiosity as I walked back toward her. She had already given me so much just by helping me through my biopsy. The lady smiled as she pulled out her card and began to write on the back. She smiled as she said, "If you ever need anything while you are here, do not be scared to give me a call."

That lady did not know me from Adam before I walked into her exam room. Despite our lack of acquaintance, she had treated me as if I was her own son. That wonderful woman might have acted like that on a regular basis, but it made me think. Why does it take such hard situations for people to show how wonderful they are to each other? More specifically than that, why did *I* need to be put in such an awkward situation for me to see how wonderful people are?

CHAPTER EIGHTEEN

Seeing Things for the First Time

§

Have mercy on me, O God, according to Your unfailing love; according to Your great compassion blot out my transgressions. Wash away all my iniquity and cleanse me from my sin. -Psalm 51:1-2

It is not only people we do not see in life. Mud covers the eyes of men and they walk around like they can see. There is a dark coating that covers the pain through which we see our whole lives. The dark pain obstructing one's view is caused by the *movie effect*. I first noticed the *movie effect* because I have such a great love for the cinema. I was leaving the movies one afternoon when I asked myself why I liked watching movies so much. Is it not interesting we will sit and watch the imaginary lives of people and laugh, cry, and love in ways that seem impossible in everyday life? There is a certain feeling of happy relaxation that comes as we watch the lives of imaginary people unfold in the cinema.

The audience of a movie sits and watches a film through an emotionally clean lens. The characters in a story do not have to deal with the baggage people bring to relationships in real life. The person watching the movie is outside him or herself as he or she watches and he or she is happy to be there. I do not believe it is a disdain for one's self that causes the sensation of being out of reality to be appealing. I believe it is the need to be clear of the mud.

A person watching a movie is uninvolved with the dirt that is upon him. A spectator cleans his or her eyes so that he or she might see the story unfold. The mud that is cleared off the eyes is full of self-consciousness, greed, lust, pride, and guilt. It is guilt and pride that draw most of the mud toward people. The *movie effect* causes people to take themselves out of the equation. When people are not involved in the story which is unfolding, there is little guilt or pride to draw mud over the way they see the world.

***

The mud was beginning to be stripped from my eyes as I left the hospital and headed home. I had made it through all the tests and I was on my way back to start my treatments. My dad had asked for Dr. Hart to send his orders to a doctor in Victoria so I could be closer to home. I was going to get treatment at the hospitals at which my dad worked. I was very thankful to be able to take my treatment at home. I knew I would get special treatment at home and I was really ready to leave Houston. M.D. Anderson is a wonderful place that saves lives and even though I knew that, it still shot fear through me like I did not think possible. With every patient I encountered, I feared what would happen to me and I thought about all the pain they were suffering. I was very glad to leave as we pulled onto the freeway.

I called my girlfriend on the way home and let her know I would be back in town. I thought about all the things at home I had missed. As we drove, I was so glad to be out of the situation I had found myself in a few days earlier. I had no greater hope I would live. In fact, I had all the more reason to fear I would die, and yet that possibility was not what was on my heart.

There was a sense of joy that filled me as we drove. I had been in some very hard situations and the Lord had allowed me to make it through. I did not just make it through, I was helped along the way. It is an amazing feeling when one's eyes are opened and one realizes he is going to be lifted out of the pit in which he finds himself. Even if someone is still in the bottom of the pit, simply knowing another person is outside the pit willing to help him get out that can change the way in which he sees everything.

It is hope that brightens the hearts of hurting men. I had experienced hope in a whole new way after that weekend at M.D. Anderson. I was not better, as far as physical ailments went, but I had a new hope. I realized my faith had a deeper facet than I had experienced before. When I was scared and death was at my door, God sent people to pull me out. I realized on a level deeper than cerebral knowledge that God was not going to leave me. Through all the pain I was to encounter, God would send people to minister to me. There is a hope people gain in knowing God will not leave or forsake them that is better than being healed.

As we drove home, I noticed I could see God's presence all around me. Sometimes it looked a lot like my fellow man, but it was His work. The presence of God brings with it something wonderful. There is a peace and happiness in the presence of God that can be found nowhere else. God stretches beyond the depths of imagination and has the power to change things in a word. It would be His strength that encouraged someone to the state of euphoria if it was not for His love. The Lord's love is more wonderful than finding favor in the arms of a beautiful woman. Anytime I saw a beautiful woman looking at me, I was filled with satisfaction at the fact someone so pretty would like me. Now, I cannot help but think how much more astounding is it God finds us attractive. God is more beautiful than any girl in the world, and yet God would love me? It is in this wonderful mystery one finds the greatest joy.

I drove home as a man in love. A man or woman in love glows like no ordinary person. When great love catches him or her by the heart, there is newness to life that was not there before. It was as we pulled into the small town of Cuero it dawned on me how much my view of the world had changed.

There is a hill in Cuero that stretches across the eastern side of the town. This hill is nothing spectacular, but from its height the rest of the town below can be seen. There are trees blocking some of the view, but the trees are more like a rich green lining. The trees highlight the main road that leads into town from the east. It was on this road, atop this hill, we drove as we came home. Cuero was always a stepping stone in my mind. The town was small and I saw nothing particularly redeeming about it as I grew up. For the most part, kids saw Cuero as a cage they were kept in until they were old enough to fly away.

I definitely felt caged as I grew up. It seemed Cuero could never be the place where I found true success. I knew Cuero offered a stage to propel me into achievement, but it was not a place where success lay. The world told me my entire life if I was to be the "All-American Boy", if I was to be successful, it would be found outside the confines of a small, South Texas town. All the things life told me I wanted: money, women, and fame– they were all found in moving myself to bigger and better places. It was the allure of being the best that drew people to a person, and I knew the best was not Cuero.

I descended that hill and realized something. It was subtle and not well thought out, but it was smoldering in the back of my mind. I saw the trees pass by my window as I drove and I loved them. The sun was bright and just breaking behind some clouds and I felt alive. There was something sweet in the air in my mind as we descended into the town in which I thought I could not be happy. There was joy in my heart and I found it in Cuero. It was not Cuero I found it in as much as it was a sense of surrounding. I was surrounded by the hand of God. It was not because I wanted to be surrounded by God, but it was because He wanted me to be.

Knowing He would pull me out if I fell, knowing He loved me enough to go to such lengths to comfort me, had changed the way I saw all that surrounded me. I could have been anywhere and been happy. It did not matter where I went, God was going to be there with me and that is why everything looked different. The world looked better. I did not want everyone to know me or be the best in anything. I just wanted to sit, to live, to be with God and His people. I wanted to garden! I was 18 years old and I wanted to garden! Gardening was the sort of thing that looked different now. Everything I thought was boring and unprofitable before now looked appealing.

I wanted to hear people's stories. I had not wanted to hear people's stories before. It had seemed like a great waste of time. Their stories were not going to help me out of the pits in which I found myself. People's stories

could not take me to success. I came down that hill realizing something that struck my soul with a dynamite
force. The stories of people were the key to my success.
There were people all around me who were being pulled
out of the dreadful situations of life all the time.

Every story I heard reminded me of how much God
loved me. Every story someone was willing to share with
me reminded me God was here to pull us out. God was
my success story. God was the one who was going to
love me. Every desire I had for the world was some queer
shadow of a desire God wanted to fulfill in my life. The
shadows had seemed so real before. I guess when one's
eyes are covered in filth, it is hard to tell what is real and
what is not.

I came home to Cuero, Texas that day and I came
home with the joy of realizing I had been saved. There
were so many years through which I lived being saved,
and yet it was not until right then that I felt it. I had been
cleansed with the baptism of pain and I was thankful for
my sight. I know pain is not a popular topic in our world,
but I will not apologize for it. It was good for me. I was a
conceited, self-righteous, and ungrateful child and I
needed to be slapped around.

I would try to praise God for every hardship that
came my way after that. There are times when things
need to be hard, because if they are not, we become fat,
lazy, and ungrateful. It was the martyrs who solidified
Christianity in the early years and it will be martyrs who
sustain it in our later years. It is not always flesh that

needs to die. It is not always flesh that is hardest to give up. There are brave men who die, but there are braver men who allow themselves to die and then decide to get back up and live. There was much pain to come in my life before I saw this truth.

CHAPTER NINETEEN

It Was Found in the Lowest of Lows

§

My heart is in anguish within me; the terrors of death assail me. Fear and trembling have beset me; horror has overwhelmed me. -Psalm 55:4-5

It was sweet to be home. The comfort and familiarity of the smell of my living room was something I had longed for while I was in the hospital. Our living room at home always has the same scent. It is a scent that is unique to our house and it reminded me of childhood every time I smelled it. My stay in the comforts of home did not last long before I had to go back to the hospital, but this time in Victoria. I had my first chemotherapy treatment and I was nervous, but not terribly nervous. We left home early a few days after returning home from

Houston. I hated getting up early, and I especially hated to get up and go do something that I did not want to do.

Despite my resistance, my mother dragged me to Victoria. It was an anxious car ride for the entire twenty minutes. I did not know what to expect and the worst was on my mind. After arriving at the hospital, we made our way through the lobby and asked for directions to the oncology wing of the hospital. We found the right elevator and made our way the appropriate floor.

The elevator doors opened and as we exited something hit me that would be all too familiar and unforgettable later. If the smell of my living room was bliss, the smell that hit me as I walked out of that hospital elevator was the stench of torture. Life is a series of smells! Some smells fill a person with delight and warmth, like the smell of one's grandmother's cooking as one gets up in the morning. Other smells remind us of victory and fun, like the smell of freshly cut grass on the baseball diamond. There are smells that will make us dizzy with the thoughts of love. Certain perfumes that remind me of my first infatuations can still make me sweat with just a little hint of their scent. Life is a series of smells because life is a wonderful array of experiences. The smell that came as I stepped off that hospital elevator was one that will be forever etched into my mind. It was the smell of sterilization. The smell of medicine, alcohol, and cleaners came together in a wretched breeze.

My mom and I made our way down the hall to the oncology department. It was in the oncology department, among all the horrid smells, that the freshest breeze I have ever encountered greeted us. She was my nurse and would be my nurse for my entire treatment process. Her name was Diane and she was originally from Canada. She had very blonde hair and was a small, elegant woman. Looking back, I remember her to be quite beautiful. I believe her to have been a good-looking woman on first encounter, but it was what radiated from her that made her so gorgeous. She was the happiest person I had ever met. The things we went through together were never happy and yet she never wavered in her enthusiasm and encouragement. She held my soul in her hands and breathed wonderful life into me.

There were a series of protocols we had to go through before I could start my treatment, but it was not long before I found myself in a hospital bed. The first treatment was different from all the others. The first chemotherapy treatment required me to spend the night in the hospital. I was not opposed to staying the night at the hospital as I was pretty scared and unsure about what treatment was going to be like.

The night I spent in the hospital was different than any other previous experience. I was only in the hospital that one night and I made both my parents go home. They had done so much already and I did not see much point in them sitting up at the hospital with me. My pastor from home stopped by my room for a minute and tried to encourage me. The effort was appreciated, but after he left it was lonely and the treatment still awaited me.

The nurses came into my room and hooked me up to a number of I.V. lines. I had a Mediport® implanted in my chest, which was used to administer the chemo drugs. The Mediport® was a metal disc with a rubber nipple that was used as a reservoir. It had an I.V. coming off of it, which was inserted into one of my arteries. The Mediport® was completely under the skin and allowed me to take baths and things of that nature normally. In order to hook me into the I.V., the nurses would take a very strange needle, which was small and had a butterfly -type handle on it, and they would cram the needle through my skin and into the reservoir. I soon found that among my nurse's very redeeming qualities, she was really good at hooking me into my chemo treatment.

I was a little nervous as the bags of chemicals continued to be hung up. I somehow expected it to be really awful as soon as the bags were connected to me, but it was not. I waited for something to happen, but nothing did for a while. It was not until a few hours later I was hit by something. I had been comfortably situated in my bed with covers pulled up all around me. Covers are a very necessary commodity when spending a lot of time in a hospital. I always wondered why hospitals felt the need to freeze sick people to death. I later found out the temperature is for the machines running in the hospital and for situations like surgery where doctors might get sweaty.

Despite the low temperature, I was not cold at all under my multitude of blankets. As I watched television, however, I began to feel like it was getting a lot colder in the room. I did not want to say anything to the nurses because I knew it was always cold in hospitals. I sat in my bed and got colder and colder until I was shaking uncontrollably. I could not stop shaking and I was shaking so hard my bed was moving on the tile floor. My body started to ache and sweat.

A few minutes later my nurse came running in the room and began to administer something through my I.V. After the convulsions were over, I was given a slightly stern talking to about not letting the nurses know how I was doing. I did not mean to be secretive, I just did not realize what was happening until it was happening. The convulsions were scary, but they were over in a fairly short period of time and I was no worse for wear. The short period of my body shaking was about the worst thing I encountered during my stay in the hospital.

My mom showed up to get me the next day, and I was up and dressed and ready to go home. I could not believe people made such a big deal about these chemo treatments. It was not that bad at all. I could handle six months of this with no problem. I was smiling and felt fine, but my nurse was giving my mom medicine to take with us and kept saying I should take it easy. I did not understand what the medicine was for because I did not feel bad in the least. I had decided I was going back to school that very same day. My nurse said it was not a good idea, but I tried to tell her I would be fine.

We left the hospital and started to drive home. I was chipper and telling my mom how great I felt as we drove. I had her stop to get me some water because my mouth was dry and I knew the doctors said dry mouth would be one of the side effects. I did not care about dry mouth, it was nothing a little water could not fix. We stopped at a convenient store to get something to drink.

I got out of the car to stretch my legs. As I stood up, a wave of nausea came on me so fast I did not have time to react. I wobbled down to the side of the car and grabbed my stomach. My mom was inside and as she paid for the water, I made my way back into the front seat. I sat there for a moment as my head spun. All of a sudden, I felt really sick to my stomach. I thought to myself, *Be strong!* but it was no use. I could not be strong. I opened the car door and started to throw up. My mom made her way back to the car, took one look at me, and reached for the bottle of medicine. She was opening up the bottle as I said, "Mom, I do not feel so good." Mom nodded in agreement and handed me a pill to take. I took that pill and a journey down a path I had never been before began.

The lowest place one can find one's self is at the point where death seems better than life. It is a hard place to get to and it is an even harder place in which to be. There, among the contemplations of the mind, a question was asked, *What is this life you live?* For the next five days, I would find myself on a path leading me to the lowest place in all humanity.

CHAPTER TWENTY

The Shadow Begins to Move

§

But David's men said to him, "Here in Judah we are afraid. How much more, then, if we go to Keilah against the Philistine forces!" Once again David inquired of the Lord and the Lord answered him, "Go down to Keilah, for I am going to give the Philistines into your hand." -1 Samuel 23:3-4

Men take many steps in this life while never seeing the ground upon which they walk. Humanity is a race of people with stubbed toes and disoriented minds. The path we tread is not as dangerous as the lack of light we allow to be shed upon it. The first eclipse I ever saw was in a book and yet it was a frightening thing. The sun was something so big and powerful, and yet for a moment it was blocked out of sight. The idea of a day that had been bright to suddenly have a giant shadow covering it seemed very strange and scary.

There is something scary about the darkness. The idea of not being able to see one's world is a frightening proposition. As a child and as an adult, the darkness presents an image from which to run. It is when one cannot run anymore, and the darkness seems to overtake a person, that the ability to stop and look for light becomes a necessity.

There is a gift in calamity. It is the clarity of mind to see the true nature of a situation. People may be blinded by an absence of light, but it is a self-imposed darkness. The hearts of men have experienced an eclipse of the divine design. If only people would stop running in the shadow and instead, unplug their ears, soften their hearts, and search for the light waiting for a chance to shine brightly beyond the reach of the objects desiring to impede it. If only men could see, if only men could hear, all the wonderful things the Lord will bring when He is near.

***

I felt I was deep within a shadow as I rolled back and forth on my bed. I had never felt so much pain in my life nor have I experienced anything like it since. My bed was really comfortable, but as I thrashed around, it felt like the hardest thing upon which I had ever lay. I moved to one side and it seemed to be like a sauna, but as soon as I moved to the other it felt the same way. The heat of my body seemed to be trapped in the bed no matter into which section of the bed I rolled. I tried to think of somewhere nice. Thoughts of beaches struck my mind. Maybe a cool breeze and a nice ocean mist. Those were good thoughts and I hoped they would distract me.

I never made it to the refreshing frozen drink because a sharp pain shot through my stomach. I curled up into the fetal position, hoping it would pass. If I could just wait it out, it would not last forever. I kept telling myself, *It will pass, just hold on!* The pain started sharp and then seemed to roll around my entire body. My forehead was sweating and I only wanted to avoid each previous position in which I had found myself for the last twenty-four hours. It was too much and I could not help it as I rolled off the side of my bed and began to throw up. I heaved as hard as I could, but it was no use. I had already thrown up too much. There was nothing in my stomach and my body just heaved, wishing it could throw up all my insides.

It was only the first day after chemotherapy and I was sure the pain would subside soon. It was a vicious cycle of throwing up and feeling better, only to realize the sensation of ease would be gone in minutes. I thought the cycle would stop, but it just went on and on. I had been really weak before the chemo and it rocked my body to the bones. It always seemed like the nights were worse than the days. There was some temporary relief to be found in sleep, but it was the sharp interruption of sleep that brought the greatest pain. All of a sudden, I would find myself awake and bent in half by pain. There was a sweat that would develop in my sleep and it seemed to remind me of how much I was hurting.

Even at age 18, there is a reaction that occurs when one is found to be in great need. I would awaken from sleep and the pain would take me straight to my parents' bedroom. I knew they could not make the pain stop, but there was something inside of me that knew they needed to know. It felt like if they shared the pain with me, it would not hurt as bad. I would make my way to my dad's side of the bed and lightly shake him. I could not stand upright as I talked to him and I was just barely higher than the top of the mattress as I talked. It was a reoccurring pattern that happened almost every night after my chemotherapy. After I woke Dad up, I would say in a really feeble voice, "Dad, I do not feel very good."

He would look at me, a little sleepy and concerned, and say, "Okay, Son, let's get you back in bed." I never made it back to bed. There was a series of steps that led out of the living room in our house. Every part of the house was accessible from the living room, but every part had a couple of steps that needed to be climbed in order to get out of the sunken living room. It never failed as I crossed the steps into the living room I would fall down onto my knees. I just could not go any further and I would find myself heaving on all fours.

Dad would reach for a small trash can that was always close by and would hold me as my body shook. It may seem silly that I asked my dad to come and watch me throw up, but it helped more than I can explain. Dad would get a wet washcloth and press it to the back of my neck as I writhed back and forth. I would continue in this fashion until little blood vessels popped all over my face, causing little red dots all over my face and eyes. Dad must have grown so tired all those nights of getting up and watching me be sick, and yet he always got up.

There is something very important in what my dad did for me all those nights. He did not fix the pain for me because he could not, but he did all he could. Dad got up every night and shared my pain. There is no way to take someone's pain upon one's self, but it is very possible to let someone know he or she is not alone on the path. There is a tendency for people to run away from hard situations and I saw that inclination when I was sick.

I understand the desire to want to run from pain, but with so much pain in the world, it seems people must overcome their fear of pain. No matter how strong someone thinks he is, there comes a point at which he breaks. There must be people, disciples of our Lord Jesus Christ, who say, "We are not scared to walk the path of pain and we will not let you break!" On one's knees with a towel in hand and the vomit of poisoned people all around is the true home of a Christian. The poison is many times different than chemotherapy, but it is poison nonetheless. Where are the hurting in the world? Find them! Without help, they will break!

Despite my dad's help, I found myself about to break. I woke up the fifth day after my chemotherapy and the pain was not gone. The vomiting had slowed, but my mouth felt like it was on fire. The chemo had cause many of my saliva glands to die and my whole mouth felt like it was turning to ash. I made my way out of the bedroom and into the living room.

As I crawled out onto the living room couch, I was a pale ghost of my former self. My parents both looked at me with pain-stricken eyes and I was in turmoil as I sat looking back at them. I did not want to let out what it was I was feeling, but I could not help but do so. Sitting on the couch, I began to cry as my parents tried to comfort me. I tried to blubber out, "I am going to die."

Dad looked at me and tried to be reassuring, telling me "You are not going to die."

I kept crying and looked at him with all the seriousness I could muster. "You do not understand!" I cried, "I cannot live like this! I cannot make it any longer like this. I would rather die than live like this for six months."

My parents both said it had to get better soon, but I was not so sure and I just cried until I did not have any emotion left.

I lay in my bed that day not knowing if I was going to live or die. I always said if I was faced with death, I would be strong and courageous, but now that I felt like it was close to me, I was not strong or courageous. I was scared and mad. I was mad at myself and scared I would not have another chance to live life. There were so many things I still wanted to do. My girlfriend's brother had a baby about the time I got sick, and I loved that little girl so much. I could not bear the idea I might never have a daughter of my own. I might never have a wife or a family. I had not seen much of the world, but none of these possible realities made me as sad as what I was soon to realize about myself.

As I lay in my bed with the uncertainty of my situation strangling me, I felt like I could not breathe, I could not hope, and I could not go on without reassurance. I was desperate and in desperation, I prayed with all my heart. I knew God usually spoke through subtlety, but that was not good enough at the moment. I needed an answer or I was not going to be able to push through. I cried out to God with all I had, "Father, answer me! I need to hear from You now. It will not do for me to wait it out and try and discern your answer. I need to hear You, to really hear Your voice."

I sat in silence waiting for Him to come. I was not going to move until I felt He was thick in the room. I knew He would come. He had to come because He loved me. I waited while my mind searched for a place where we might meet. *Where was He?* I needed Him so much as I lay there anxiously awaiting His presence.

I do not know if it was minutes or hours, but eventually He came, or maybe it is better to say I found Him. My soul bent to its knees, although my knees could not bend. After a few minutes, I got up the courage to ask the question that was tearing my heart apart. It was a question that still brings a knot into my throat and a question that shook my whole body to ask, "Father, am I going to die?" The words seemed to reach into a vast canyon and echo back into my heart as I spoke them. I needed the answer so much, and yet I was so scared to receive it. I waited and nothing came, so I called out again, "Father, I need to know, am I going to die?"

It was not audible so anyone else in the house could hear it, but it was the loudest answer I have ever felt in my life. It seemed to resonate throughout my entire body and moved my emotions into a frenzy. The word shot through me like an arrow, *YES!*

Tears started to flow and my body trembled as tears ran down my face. I was going to die, how could this be? It was not the life I had hoped for or envisioned as I was growing up. Why would God do this to me? All the things I had not been able to do yet were mounting in my mind, and then it hit me, *What about all the things I should have done?* All the people I went to high school with began to run through my head. There were so many people I had not paid attention to. There were so many people I had wronged and so many people with whom I had not shared the Lord. I knew I was going to heaven, but what I had to leave on Earth was more than I could bear.

All the times God had called me to serve Him began to run through my head. Why had I not answered His call? Why had I not done what I knew I should do? I had spent all my life chasing success through the ways the world told me to and now none of it mattered. Was I the "All-American Boy?" Was I what everyone expected me to be? I did not know and I did not care, because as I lay on that bed, I realized I was not all God wanted me to be and He was the only one I had left.

Desperation over took my soul as I realized soon everything I had worked for would be gone and everything I had ignored would be important. The tears that poured from my eyes were from so many different things that it is impossible to describe. The tears coursed from my eyes, but they were only a sprinkle compared with the tears that poured from my heart, down through my soul and into my gut where they accumulated into a lake of regret and fear.

I made my way out of bed and into the living room where my dad was sitting. He looked up at me with my face flushed with tears. I looked at him and said, "Dad, God told me I was going to die."

Dad looked at me and asked, "What do you mean God told you that you were going to die?"

I was trying not to cry, but I was not succeeding as I said, "I was praying and I asked God if I was going to die and He said, 'Yes.'"

My father looked at me with wiser eyes than I had and said, "Well, go back and pray some more."

I did not know what else to do and it sounded like a good idea so I went back to my bed. I got on my knees in my bed and curled up in a ball under the covers. I sat there until I was ready to talk and then I began a discussion that would change my life forever.

"Father, why do I have to die?" I felt like there was no question I could not ask. He was my God and He had loved me my whole life despite myself. I continued on in discussion as I waited for a reply, "I do not want to die, Father! Why do I have to die?" I sat searching for Him, waiting for an answer.

It was not long before my response came in the same form that it had earlier. The words seemed to turn the universe upside down. There is an easy way to tell what I am talking about. Find a map of the world and study it for a while. After the map seems familiar, go to a local Outback Steakhouse and look at the map they have on the wall. There should be a map of the world with Australia on top. If there is not an Outback close by, or if they do not have the picture, find a map on the internet with the world upside down and look at it. There is no reason why Australia should be on the bottom, but it always is. There is no up or down in space, but we have always seen Australia on the bottom of our maps. It is the same planet that appears on the upside down map and it really is not upside down, but it looks so much different. It is as if the world is a whole new place with Australia on top instead of on the bottom.

The map of my world had always had God on the bottom with the hopes of my world on top. The Lord's response to my question changed the way I saw the world.

In the quiet after my question, the Lord spoke up, *Every-one dies, Andrew. Why do you worry about that which you do not control? Why do you not just do what I ask of you?*

A peace settled in my heart as I let the response of my God marinate in my heart. He was right and I was so silly. Jesus Christ loved me and I loved Him and that fact was all that mattered. I did not need to worry about when I would die, because I knew someday I would die. It was not knowing when I would die that caused me to change the way I felt about life. Something in the Lord's answer told me I would not die right that second and I had the rest of my life to live what He was asking me to do.

I knew what I lived for now. People had told me my whole life I had to live for Jesus Christ alone, but I never knew what they meant until that exact moment in my bed. All the fame and glory I had wanted was nothing that mattered when I thought my life was going to be over. I wanted so much for people to think well of me when I was growing up, but as I fought against dying, I did not care what people thought. I no longer looked like a good athlete. I was literally wasting away and yet I did not care one bit. There was only one person whose opinion I cared about and He was Jesus Christ. He did not care what accomplishments I had accumulated, nor did He care what I looked like physically. I lay on my deathbed and realized the only thing my Lord cared about was that I loved Him enough to do what He asked of me.

216 | ANDREW B. HEARD

How did I go for so long without showing Him that love? I loved Him so much and I had chased other things for so long without heeding His call. One might think I would be sucked back into regret at this point, but that was not the case at all. Jesus Christ is the most wonderful savior, because He understands us so much better than we ever understand ourselves. I was not regretful, because in my tears, I had asked for forgiveness. I was crying for the Lord to forgive me for my infidelity and He heard my prayer.

A sense of peace came over me more wonderful than anything a man can experience in this life. I was no longer sad about all the things I did not do, nor all the things I might not get to do. I was at peace because from that point on, no matter for how long it might be, I had the chance to make God proud of me. I had the chance to do what He asked of me and to love Him with all my heart, all my soul, and all my mind.

All the dreams of becoming the "All-American Boy" were gone. The accolades that came with that title would never last the fires of death and they meant nothing to me. I only wanted for the Lord to say, "Well done, my good and faithful servant." How could I have wanted anything else? Jesus Christ was my one great love and He always had been. I had been distracted most of my life, but He was always there and I should have always shown Him I loved Him. There were so many people who did not know the love I had because I did not show the love I felt for Christ. A new day dawned in my life that day. It was a dawn filled with a love song so sweet death could not overcome it.

CHAPTER TWENTY-ONE

Slaying the Myth

§

**So David triumphed over the Philistine
with a sling and a stone; without a sword
in his hand he struck down the Philistine
and killed him. -1 Samuel 17:50**

There are Goliaths we must slay. The giants that
stand before us are not flesh, but they are just as
large and as intimidating as any earthly creature could be.
The giants of our world stand at the front of life's battle
lines and call out to us. The call is powerful and threatens
everything God-fearing men would stand for; it is a
mocking taunt of what Christ would call us to be.

The myths of ancient days gave a framework through
which people could view their world. There were gods
for every encounter man might have on earth. If someone was lost at sea, it was because he had angered Poseidon and Poseidon had decided to avenge himself upon
that person. These myths governed people's lives and

struck fear into the hearts of men. Through the stories of gods, men saw their lives and their meaning.

Myths appear to be stories of long ago that people believed because they did not know any better, but myths are not so outdated. A modern myth has been promulgated upon society and it strikes fear into the hearts of men just as ancient sea gods did. The modern myth drives the paradigm of men just as much as any ancient poem of Homer ever did.

The modern myth is indeed a way to see the world and a means to spend one's life pursuing, but it is also just a myth. The modern myth is found in the young men of America and many other countries around the world. The giant of the modern myth does not have a sword or a spear, but it is armed with expectations. The modern myth is full of the unsatisfying expectations of imaginary accomplishment. The accomplishments are indeed imaginary and they are many of the hopes of the "All-American Boy".

Young men and women seek fame and approval in the eyes of their fellow men, eyes that can bring no true reward. The modern myth tells people to seek security in self-advancement, that if they seek what is best for them, then they will find true fulfillment in having reached the top. The modern myth is a cry to find love in things that can never bring one true love. All the things the modern myth tells us to seek are a search for love. The pursuit of self-advancement and fame are both desperate pursuits to try and obtain love through the admiration of one's fellow man. The endeavors of men to fulfill the American Dream of 401K's and owning one's own house are attempts to find love.

The man who tries more than anything to accumulate security is the man who wants more than anything to love and enjoy life without the hassles of stress and the burdens of being without. The giant calls men to find love in the arms of women. I say the "arms" of women, because it is not the heart to which the modern myth calls us. To find love in a woman's heart is a beautiful endeavor, but it is beautiful because it is the bonding of two souls. There is a union of souls that occurs between a man and a woman that resembles the divine relationship humanity has with God.

To penetrate someone to the very core of who he or she is and have a union of emotion and spirit is a reminder of the Christian's encounter with God. The true encounter is more than just sex; it is binding in an eternal fashion the modern myth knows nothing about. There is no love in the pursuit of lust, only a cheap imitation which provides no true satisfaction. The list of things the modern myth tells us will fill our heart's void and bring us true love is endless. I thought sports, fame, and women would bring me what my heart desired, but the range of things which men will try and replace God with is endless.

Every attempt to satisfy the craving of the heart for love outside of Jesus Christ is futile. There are many things in this life that are good, but none endure without

Christ Jesus. All the pursuits of life outside the spectrum of Christ are shadows of true love. True love can only be truly present as long as one continues to inhabit it. To have true love for a moment, and then to be without it is not to have obtained it, but to have only tasted what could have been.

Shadows resemble an object, but they are not the object themselves. It is nice to look at shadows and how they resemble the features of the object they represent, but when one tries to grab the shadow it simply slips away. It is a sad thing to watch a person chase that which was never really there. To run with great effort, and never satisfy the desire of one's heart is something most men endure at one time or another, but the race always comes to an end.

Life comes to an end for all men, for all men die. It is on one's deathbed the question is asked, "Have I obtained what I longed for? Is love something I possess?" Those who have sought fulfillment in the lies of the modern myth will find the answer too much to bear, just as I did. The men who sought fame will find there is no one to cheer them on when they are dead. The men who sought security will find there is no security that will protect them from death. The life they wanted so much to love will be taken from them no matter how much money they have. The men that sought love in the arms of women will find no woman's arms await them when they die. All that was sought in the lives of men without Jesus Christ will fade away in death, and the shadows men chased will haunt them for eternity. A shadow does not quench the thirst of the heart and the desperation of a dry soul.

The giant may not be flesh and blood, but it is very much alive and it breathes out blasphemous lies from all directions. The fight of men is hard, for the voice of opposition is so loud. The definition of success is blasted by the modern myth through every available means of communication. The movies we watch portray the successful through earthly measurements which distort the truth of a successful pursuit. The guy who gets the girl and wins the football game is the successful man, but his success is not followed to the finish. The greatest draw of the modern myth is the use of snapshot advertisement.

If taken in pieces, any product can look appealing. A car without an engine looks really nice until one tries to drive it. A movie can look like a blockbuster from the preview, but in the course of an entire film one may find the preview just showed the best parts. The modern myth may show a life that touches something that resembles love, but it is perseverance that determines the true nature of love. Was the love of the young man in the movie for his girl and his victory still present at the hour of his death?

All men seek love and all men seek God. Everything that resembles love, but fades away, is something that resembles God. Every good thing is from God and therefore everything good men seek is a search for God. Men wander through stories and myths looking for God, and yet they only find poor shadows. It is when men who know the true God purposefully choose to lift up the shadows as their god instead that society falls into the hands of evil thoughts.

I was guilty of lifting up shadows before God took ahold of my life through the pain of cancer and the beauty of testing that brought out my foolishness. I was an idolater! I thought football, girls, and fame would bring me love, while knowing the whole time the One who gave me true love. My actions dictated to the world I thought things other than God would bring me love and that made me an idolater. I loved the stories of men more than the Words of God.

How long will those who know the love of Jesus Christ stand by and honor the passing love of the modern myth? It must be the heart of every saint to admire the man who listens to the commands of Jesus Christ and not those who heed the call of the world. It is the man who loves the Lord and loves his neighbor as himself who is a success in this life. It is the man who goes unnoticed turning on the church lights who is the success, and not the lawyer who does anything to win, despite the moral implications of his actions.

CHAPTER TWENTY-TWO

Your Best Life Later

§

For God so loved the world that He gave His one and only Son, that whoever believes in Him shall not perish but have eternal life. - John 3:16

I have told my story to many people over the last six years. Each time, I give a more concise version of the story which I just recounted on these pages. Many times at the end of the story people are very moved, but there is one question I almost always forget to answer: Am I still sick? I have not died at the age of 24, since I am writing this story and speaking about it, but it is not clear yet whether or not I am well. It would seem like a great testament of God's greatness to be able to say with complete certainty I am fully healed and I have gone on to see great success on the football field and in life. Many people would see that as a way to sell a good story, but that is not my story and that is not why I have written this book.

I am medically cured of cancer. I have played college football for two Division I football teams: Texas Tech University and Baylor University. It would seem God has truly blessed me by giving me health and success. The truth is, God has done extraordinary things in my life, but it all starts with death. The day I prayed to God and asked Him if I was going to die and He said, *Yes*, I really did die. The truth is I die every day and that is the only way I can truly live. In Galatians 2:20 Paul says:

I have been crucified with Christ and I no longer live, but Christ lives in me. The life I live in the body I live by faith in the Son of God who loved me and gave Himself up for me.

As God talked to me that day on my bed, the message He was sharing with me was one of crucifixion. Taking up one's cross means dying to what the Self wants and giving up everything for what God wants. Slaying the myth starts with dying to ourselves. The idea of dying to one's self is completely opposite of what the world tells us, but it is exactly what the Scripture tells us. Paul tells us in Romans 6:1-4:

What shall we say, then? Shall we go on sinning so grace may increase? By no means! We died to sin; how can we live in it any longer? Or do not you know all of us who were baptized into Christ Jesus were baptized into His death? We were therefore buried with Him through baptism into death in order that, just as Christ was raised from the dead through the glory of the Father, we, too, may live a new life.

When I said the myth is not new, what I really meant is it is as old as creation. The sin Paul talks about dying to is Self. The first sin described in the Garden of Eden was the sin of Self. Eve thought she could become like God. Eve believed the myth that her satisfaction could be found in trying to sustain her own life and happiness. Our sin is the same as Eve's sin; we believe we should run our own life and that we do not desire the things of God. In the end, the myth leads only to death. The good news of the gospel is if we die to Self we will live with Christ through His resurrection. Christ never believed the myth we chase and yet He died. His death and resurrection mean we, too, can have life and have it to the fullest.

The idea that Christ brings life to the fullest is nothing new. For thousands of years, people have believed if we make the gods happy, then they will bless our life on earth. This idea has even been prevalent in Christian Scripture. There were many reasons I used the Old Testament passages recounting the story of David, but one of the main reasons was because of the theological thrust that many people see in these passages. The Old Testament tells us in many places, and people read into it in many places, God will bless us with physical victory and riches if we obey Him. This was, and is, one of the most prominent ideas about our relationship with God. The New Testament changes this line of thinking.

Christ does not call the Christian to obey because He will bless us with earthly treasure. In fact, Christ came to turn this idea upside down. All throughout the Scripture the question of why evil men prosper and good men die was questioned. The entire book of Job was written for this reason. Men had decided in Christ's time and still think today that those with much in this life are blessed by God. Christ's call was for men to stop looking so short-sided and realize the truth. Christ wanted men to have real life and He knew the only way they would reach real life was by dying to Self. This is most clearly illustrated in Matthew 19:16-26:

> Just then a man came up to Jesus and asked, "Teacher, what good thing must I do to get eternal life?"
> "Why do you ask me about what is good?' Jesus replied. "There is only One who is good. If you want to enter life keep the commandments."
>
> "Which ones?" he inquired.
>
> Jesus replied, "'You shall not murder, you shall not commit adultery, you shall not steal, you shall not give false testimony, honor your father and mother, and love your neighbor as yourself.'"

"All these I have kept," the young man said. "What do I still lack?"

Jesus answered, "If you want to be perfect, go, sell your possessions and give to the poor, and you will have treasure in heaven. Then come, follow me."

When the young man heard this, he went away sad, because he had great wealth. Then Jesus said to his disciples, "Truly I tell you, it is hard for the rich to enter the kingdom of heaven. Again I tell you, it is easier for a camel to go through the eye of a needle than for the rich to enter the kingdom of God."

When the disciples heard this, they were greatly astonished and asked, "Who then can be saved?"

Jesus looked at them and said, "With human beings this is impossible, but with God all things are possible."

Peter answered him, "We have left everything to follow you! What then will there be for us?"

Jesus said to them, "Truly I tell you, at the renewal of all things, when the Son of Man sits on his glorious throne, you who have followed me will also sit on twelve thrones, judging the twelve tribes of Israel. And everyone who has left houses or brothers or sisters or fathers or mothers or wives or children or fields for my sake will receive a hundred times as much and will inherit eternal life. But many who are first will be last, and many who are last will be first.

Here in the parable of the rich man we see Jesus turning the world upside down. Heaven does not come to the rich man by keeping laws, but by giving up himself and following Christ. The rich man has to die and invest for the long term.

I have heard from many accomplished people it is better to invest long-term than it is to have all one wants now and have nothing later. This is the truth Jesus is trying to share with us: it is better to die to ourselves now and have eternal life than it is to live today and die for eternity. This is truth, but it is so hard to live because it is hard to stare into the face of poverty and death and have faith it will be worth it in the end. In a life where the good guy does not get what he deserves, it is hard to believe following Jesus will one day bring the greatest reward.

There are "Christians" who will say God wants us to have our best life now, but look at Scripture and look at life and tell me if this is true. I believe God wants us to have our best life, but I believe He wants us to have it later. Was it better for the rich man to have nothing than to be rich? It clearly was not better to give up everything in the short term, but Christ was looking with eternity in mind. Was it better for Christ to be humiliated, beaten, betrayed, and murdered on a cross at the time? No, but it was better with the future in mind, with our future in mind.

Christ does not only want us to be happy now, Christ wants us to be joyful for eternity. Christ does not want us to promote ourselves, to chase the myth. Christ does not want us to never be sick or hurt, and it is not a sign of little faith to be in a hard place. The troubles of this world are because the world has believed the lie that we do not need God. They are a condition of the world and the world must pass away and be made new for these things to be fixed.

Look to the scriptures to see if what I am saying is true. Scripture says we are to make disciples in Matthew 28:19-20. We are to be disciples and discipleship is completely contrary to the prosperity gospel that is preached in church and on television today. The word disciple means a disciplined follower of a master. Discipleship means being like Christ. Christ was never rich. Christ was a tender preacher who loved the poor and the outcasts of society. Christ was man who, instead of promoting Himself and ensuring His life was good, gave up His life and took on scorn so we might live. If the picture of Christ is not convincing enough that discipleship does not mean life is never hard, then look to what history says about the twelve disciples who followed Him. History and, granted, some myth, says all twelve of the disciples faced martyrdom. Health, wealth, and prosperity do not await us at the cross, death awaits us at the cross.

Dying for Christ and being buried in baptism is something I always heard in church and is something I never understood. How can one die for Christ? How did I die for Christ that day on my bed? I have to say Fred Cradock, a great preacher, said it better than I ever could. In a very famous sermon, Cradock said that as a boy he always envisioned dying for Christ being something very romantic. He envisioned going to somewhere in the European Eastern block and standing before a communist statue as they asked him if he believed in Jesus. Craddock said in his mind he would stand tall and announce Christ was his Savior and then they would shoot him. He always thought they would erect a stature of him there in that place and in the years to follow, they would announce very poetically that Fred Craddock had given his life there in that place.

With a smirk and a breath, Craddock, as a man approaching the end of his life, said his martyrdom was nothing like that vision. For most of us, martyrdom is never found in a moment, but instead takes our whole lives. Christ asks us to die, but this is a daily request that is not done easily in an instant. Dr. Craddock said his life was poured out, not in one big splash, but in a series of daily sips. This is the Christian call: to give up our lives in small sips every day.

It is here in the drudgery of everyday martyrdom we ask ourselves why the Christian life is worth living. I know I have asked myself this many times. One would think after an experience like I had with death and miracles, how would I ever doubt God? This is the question I used to ask about the apostles, but after living just a little I understand much better.

It is true I have played on two college football teams, but I only played four plays my whole career. It is true Christ changed me and I died on that bed, but every day I have to die again or I feel the old me coming back again. I never heard the crowd roar as I wanted to and I never proved to all the people who doubted me I was great. Is my life not perfect because I have no faith? No, but my life will be perfect because I *do* have faith.

I am alive today, but I am also dead and dying. I am dying to the myth. I am dying to myself, but I am alive in Christ! This is the Christian joy! Just as He lived, so I will live and now I have nothing to fear.

Andrew B. Heard

November 29, 1982 – July 26, 2013

The second edition of *Your Best Life Later* was created to honor my husband, Andrew B. Heard. When I met Andrew at Baylor University, he gave me the manuscript to this book after our very first date. He was re-diagnosed with cancer four years into our marriage and passed away 10 months after his diagnosis. As his wife, I have been so blessed by the way he lived his life with such character and faith, right until the very end. He inspired and shaped the woman I am today. I now travel the country sharing our family's inspirational story and the message you can embrace the lessons your challenges bring and transform them into fuel to create a more meaningful life. I also share Andrew's books, *A Gray Faith* and *The Ellie Project,* both of which he wrote in the final 10 months of his life. Andrew wrote and illustrated *The Ellie Project* for our daughter, Ellie. It contains love notes for every letter of the alphabet about the important character and life lessons he wanted to teach her throughout all her stages of growing up.

To follow our journey and see how we are keeping Andrew's legacy alive, go to: www.baileyheard.com, and to purchase Andrew's books, go to: www.ellieproject.com. If you were encouraged by this book, please share it with someone you think could benefit from it. Thank you for helping me to share Andrew's important messages with the world.

Blessings,

Bailey Heard

CPSIA information can be obtained
at www.ICGtesting.com
Printed in the USA
FSOW02n1855020216
16487FS